A History of Ireland
for Learners of English

New edition

Tony Penston

 TP Publications

TP Publications
59 Applewood Heights
Greystones, Co. Wicklow, Ireland
www.tppublications.com

First published 2010. 2019.
© Tony Penston 2019

ISBN: 978 0 9531323 4 8

Front cover (we are grateful to the relevant licensors): Same-sex marriage referendum, Getty images/C. Kilcoyne; Northern Ireland roadsign, P.J. Dunne - Cavan; Pope Francis and Taoiseach Leo Varadkar, Shutterstock; Pikemen statue, Pat Sheridan photography; The San Martín, Maritime Museum Madrid; Famine memorial Dublin, Sam Srinivasan; Croagh Patrick, EWTN photo; Viking boats, CanStockPhoto /Diomedes66; Bunratty Castle, Shannon Heritage; Equinox stone in Loughcrew, Anthony Murphy/ Mythical Ireland.com; Gold gorget, National Museum of Ireland; Brownshill Dolmen, Patricia Penston.

Back cover: Keel Village, Achill. From the Lawrence Collection, National Photographic Archive.
Cover finishing by Kevin Brooks, also artwork on pp32 & 35.
Artwork on p33 by Michael Kuntz, on p85 by Ciaran Augustine.

Thanks

To Charles Egan for his information on food supplies during the Famine. To Valerie Barry for information on the Smerwick massacre. To Karl O'Neill for information on passage tombs. To John Robbe in Willemstad, Netherlands for information on William of Orange. To Fr. Albert McDonnell of The Irish Pontifical College in Rome for information on the O'Neill and O'Donnell tombstones in Montorio. To Eddie Geoghegan of Araltas Heraldry Internet Store for information on the O'Neill coat of arms. To Roberto Piperno for information on images of Roman palaces. To Jean-Pierre Froment in Saint-Quentin, France for linguistic assistance. To Greg Rosenstock for his notes on Henry VIII. To Sue O'Donnell for information on Irish drinking habits. To Eamonn Corcoran for assistance with chapter 23. To Heinz Lechleiter for writing a section of chapter 24. To Stephen Wade for his assistance with chapter 24. To Sinéad and David O'Loghlin for the crossword. To Fareed Sababou of LAI Bray for his kind production support.

Special thanks to Fr. Frank Fahey of Ballintubber Abbey for permission to reproduce the sketch of the Chancel, also to Kerry Gibbons for her kind assistance.

Printed in Ireland by Turners Printing, Longford

Acknowledgements

We are grateful to the following for permission to reproduce copyright material (a = above; b = below; l = left; r = right; m = middle):

Abbey Theatre 76 b; AKG Images 88, & Universal Studios 102 ar; Andrew Gallimore *A Bloody Canvas* Mercier Press 96 bl; Archiseek.com 43 tr; Bayeux Tapestry Museum 22 b; British Battles.com 30 tl; Camera Press 89, 103, 104 a; Dept. of Culture, Heritage and the Gaeltacht 7 l, 8, 9 a, 11 r; David Lyons/Alamy 53 l; Donar Reiskoffer (GNU) 18 b; Examiner Publications (Denis Minihane) 63; Getty Images 16 br, 49, 68, 72, 75 a, 87 al and br, 92, 93 a, 96 a & ml, 98, 100 a, 101, 113 b; Heritage Images 36; Illustrated London News 71; Irish Linen Centre and Lisburn Museum 102 b; Irish Railway Record Society 96 mr; Jan de Fouw 20 a; Jarlath Hayes 39 l; Jeffrey L. Thomas at Castles of Wales website 23; John Kennedy/John Hinde Ltd 17 r; Jolanta Wawrzycka of Radford University VA USA 83 b; Keith Heneghan 17 al; Library of Congress Washington D.C. 67 r, 102 l; Limerick County Council 47 bl; Lough Derg Pilgrimage Centre 17 b; Maritime Museum Madrid 28; Michael Collins Association London 87 ar; National Library of Ireland 58 l, 59, 60 l; National Maritime Museum Greenwich 54 r; National Museum of Ireland 9 b, 10 b, 19, 52, 56 b, 78 b, 80, 87 bl; National Photographic Archive 57, 61, 67 l, 70, 76 a and m, 78 a, 81 b, 83 a, 84, 96 br; National Portrait Gallery 31, 45; Nick Bradshaw/Fotonic.ie 111; The O'Brien Press Ltd © 40, 43 l; P.J. Dunne - Cavan 112; Pacemaker 104 b; Press Association Images 46 b (Niall Carson), 79 bl, 105 b (Dave Caulkin); Photopress Belfast 106 l; RTÉ (TV drama) 93 b; Sportsfile 75 b; Tom Rooney 110; Trustees of National Museum Northern Ireland © 2008 National Museums Northern Ireland 30 ar & b; UCD Archives Courtesy of the UCD-OFM Partnership 79 a, 81 a; Wexford People Newspapers 51; Wolfgang & Dagmar 16 bl; Xander Clayton *Aud* GAC Press 82.

The publishers have made every effort to trace and acknowledge copyright holders. If, however, they have inadvertently overlooked any they will be pleased to make the necessary arrangements at the first opportunity.

Tony Penston has taught English and trained teachers of English for more years than he cares to remember. He now shares his time between occasional teaching, examining and writing, not neglecting his musical and other interests. His other publications include *A Concise Grammar for English Language Teachers, Essential Phonetics for English Language Teachers* and the poster, *The Articulation of Difficult Consonants*.

Introduction

A History of Ireland for Learners of English was written to facilitate the enjoyment of reading about Irish history and culture. It is most suitable for learners of English but will also find favour with native speakers who prefer a less formal style of English.

The book can be used as classroom lesson or individual reading material. When used in lesson mode it is suggested that the teacher use the normal pre-reading (question posing, visuals) and post-reading activities (question games, discussion, role-play, projects). As individual reading the book should be used in a quiet period, with dictionary access. For either mode it would be advisable to have a map of Ireland and western Europe available.

The English has been simplified roughly to an intermediate level of comprehension (B1-B2 on the Council of Europe scale). There is a progression towards C1 level (advanced) in the last few chapters.

Ideally the chapters should be read in sequence but of course they may be chosen as required with little or no detriment to understanding.

In the 'open cloze' gap-fill tasks the gaps are of different sizes to indicate somewhat the sizes of the missing words, this to follow a pedagogical principle of providing a clue where one would be provided in normal communication (length of sound, size of smudged word, etc.)

For all cloze tasks it is advisable to skim the text for gist before attempting to fill the gaps.

In the simplification process a certain licence has been necessary, for example terms such as 'English army', 'leader', etc, would otherwise require qualification. 'Governer' is used instead of 'Stadtholder', William of Orange's official title in the Netherlands. Also, detail has had to be sacrificed to a certain extent, such as the historical geography and Irish names of the provinces, etc.

A little mixing of myth with fact has been indulged to allow a full treatment of Granuaile, 'The Pirate Queen', a personage not always rated for historical works but well worth a chapter in this book. However, all other figures and events have been reported with reasonable accuracy – even St. Patrick's connection with the shamrock is deemed improbable!

I hope that benefit and enjoyment are derived from the use of this book and would appreciate comments and suggestions.

Tony Penston

Note: where the word [map] appears after the name of a place, the reader is invited to write in that place on the map in the centre of this book.

Contents

"The only history that is worth a damn is the history we make today."

Henry Ford (1863-1947)

"Those who cannot remember the past are condemned to repeat it."

George Santayana (1863-1952)

"History should not be a school subject for exams, but a discovery of knowledge for a better world."

Tony Penston

Parents of the author at a haycock in Wexford, 1940

1. THE STONE AGE

Early inhabitants
The first inhabitants of Ireland arrived about eight thousand years ago. They probably came from Scotland. These were middle stone age (mesolithic) people and were hunters. At this time the country was covered in forests and swamps, and these early hunters lived on river banks and lake shores.

The next people were late stone age (or neolithic) and were farmers. They made stone axes and with these they could cut trees. Then they were able to cultivate the land and raise cattle. They had places for religious meetings – circles of stones, and they built dolmens as graves for important people (a dolmen is a big stone with space underneath for dead people). They also built passage graves (see below).

Many of these structures show an interest in astronomy.

Circle of stones in Drombeg, Cork.
Two stones in the centre point to the setting sun on 21st December (winter solstice).

This is the main dolmen in Carrowmore, Sligo, the largest megalithic cemetery in Ireland.
It is 700 years older than Newgrange.

Passage graves
There are over 300 passage graves in Ireland. The most famous are Newgrange, Knowth and Dowth in the Boyne Valley, also Loughcrew nearby. Each consists of a mound of stones or earth with a passage leading to a central chamber. Many of the stones are carved. The carvings are mostly circular/spiral but there are also some diamonds, zig-zags and lozenges. Most of the stones were transported from the Mourne Mountains, some from the Wicklow Mountains.

[Write in 'Newgrange' and 'Mourne Mts.' on the map on pages 64-65.]

Newgrange burial mound   Passage in Newgrange

In Newgrange, once a year on 21 December the rising sun shines down the passage into the chamber for 17 minutes. Knowth contains two tombs back-to-back, with two passages, east and west. It also contains more carvings than Newgrange, in fact it is the largest gallery of megalithic art in Europe. Dowth also contains two tombs, but with one passage. The average diameter of these megalithic graves where the burnt bodies of great leaders were left is 85 metres. They are about 5,000 years old – older than the pyramids in Egypt!

For some people the mention of Egypt is not surprising: they say there is a connection with similar graves in Morocco, Portugal, Spain and Brittany (in north-west France).

Fields

The Céide Fields [map]* in Mayo, about 5,500 years old, are the oldest known field systems in the world. They extend over an area of 12 square kilometers. The fields and walls are preserved under peat (bogland), so you can't see them! Archeologists drew the map of the walls of the fields and houses by feeling them with a long iron bar! If you go there you too can feel the walls; the guide will let you stick an iron bar (over two metres long!) into the ground. The ground is soft because it is peat.

A bog is formed when the land becomes too wet to recycle the dead plants (this can be caused by cutting down too many trees). The plants in a bog die and fall into the water. In the following year the next plants do the same, building up the bog. Many people use 'turf' for their fires during the winter. Turf is cut out of the bog and dried in the summer.

*When you see [map] please write in that place on the map on pages 64-65.

Tasks (ch 1)

1. Unscramble the letters in these two words to find what was under dolmens and in passage graves: NESOB and SAESH.

2. Fill in the blanks with the words below the text:

More stone, then metal

A much later stone (a) _____ is Dún Aengus on Inishmore (the largest of the Aran Islands). It is a circular fort built on the edge of a (b) _____. It was (c) _____ defended with sharp stones all around it. There are similar (d) _____ at Grianán of Aileach near Derry and Caherdaniel in Kerry, although these do not have many stones outside.

From around 2000 BC copper and gold were (e) _____ and jewellery and implements were made. Bronze was also made from a mixture of copper and (f) _____. The tin was (g) _____ from Cornwall in England.

You (h) _____ see axe-heads and spear-heads made from bronze in the National Museum in Dublin and the Ulster Museum in Belfast.

---

forts   structure   imported   can   cliff   tin   well   mined

Dún Aengus

Grianán of Aileach

Bronze spear-heads in the National Museum of Ireland

2. CHE CELCS

Origin

The Celts arrived in Ireland around the 6th century BC. They came from central Europe, where they often fought against the Romans. Once, in 390 BC to be exact, they almost captured Rome. To Ireland they brought with them the skills of iron-making. Iron weapons are much stronger than bronze ones so the Celts easily defeated the local people. However, there is no proof of a large invasion.

The Celts were fierce warriors. They scared their enemies by sounding trumpets and shrieking. They often fought naked, and they didn't wear helmets because they wanted to show off their hair. Many of them made their hair spiky with sticky mud. Hair gel is not a new invention!

In everyday life the Celts took pride in their appearance.

Artwork by Wayne Reynolds, from the book *WAR30, Celtic Warrior 300BC-100AD*. © Osprey Publishing Ltd. www.ospreypublishing.com

They wore brightly coloured clothes and were fond of jewellery. In the National Museum in Dublin you can see some of the gold bracelets, collars and brooches that they wore. Even before the Celts there were many goldsmiths making beautiful objects in Ireland, including ornaments like the gold boat with oars that you can see in the museum.

Gold collar found in Co. Derry in 1896. It dates from the 7th century B.C.

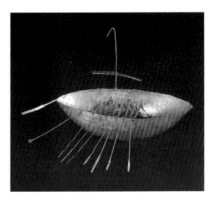

Ornamental gold boat, also found in Co. Derry in 1896. It dates from the 1st Century.

Roman expansion in Europe

The Romans conquered most of Europe, causing the Celts to change their language and culture. The Romans never came to Ireland (or Scotland) and so Celtic language and culture have survived here. Celtic language is also spoken in parts of Scotland, Wales, the Isle of Man and Brittany. In Galicia (in NW Spain) Celtic music is played on pipes.

Some Romans did come to Ireland of course, to see what it was like. The weather must have been very bad because they called the country *Hibernia,* which means 'winter' in Latin! The English spoken in Ireland is called Hiberno-English.

Hadrian's Wall, between England and Scotland, built by the Romans in 132 AD

Reconstructed crannóg (lake house) in Co. Clare

Tasks (ch 2)

1. Match the numbers with the letters:

1. The Celts used these for drinking wine.   a) armour
2. These were used instead of a knife and fork.   b) terrifying noises
3. The Celts used these to frighten their enemies. c) chariots
4. They drove into battle in these.   d) wine
5. They showed these off to their friends after a
   battle.   e) tall tales
6. Around the victory fire, they told these.   f) daggers
7. The bravest warrior received this cut of
   meat at the feast.   g) cattle horns
8. The Celts seldom wore this.   h) gold ornaments
9. They imported this from Greece.   i) heads
10. These were found in the graves of rich
    Celtic women.   j) the lion's share

2. Fill in the blanks with the words below the text:

Celtic, Gaelic, Gallic

The term 'Celtic' is a linguistic one, used to describe the people who spoke and still (a) _____ this Indo-European language. The Greeks called them *Keltoi*, the Romans, *Galli*. Gaul was the old name for (b) _____, and *Gallic* = French.

There is a (c) _____ between the names *Galicia* in Northern Spain, *Galați* in Romania, the *Galatians* in eastern Europe and Turkey, *Wales*, and of course *Galway*.

Gaelic refers to the Celtic language (d) _____ in Ireland and Scotland. It can also mean 'Irish' and it is the name for Irish football. *Gaelic* has no connection with *Gallic*. It (Gaelic) comes from the Welsh word *Guyddel* which means 'wild man'.

Dún is Celtic for 'town' or 'hill-fort', and this word can be (e) _____ in Lon<u>don</u>, <u>Dun</u>kirk, <u>Dún</u> Laoghaire, <u>Don</u>egal, <u>dun</u>es, even 'the downs', which means 'the hills' in England!

Lugh ('shining light') was the greatest of the Celtic gods and his (f) _____ can be seen in <u>Ly</u>on in France, <u>Le</u>iden in Holland, <u>Leg</u>nica in Poland, and in many mountain names in Ireland.

Ogham is a form of writing invented in Ireland around 350 A.D. It is (g) _____ on Latin letters, usually carved on gravestones. It is only suitable for short messages. Most of the early Celtic tradition was (h) _____ so we do not have written records of their history. The *seanchaí* (story-teller) tradition still exists in many places.

The Celts were not united politically. They consisted of many independent (i) _____ but they shared the same culture and beliefs. There is (j) _____ of civilization and art in Hallstatt (Austria), La Tène (Switzerland), and Heuneburg (Germany). The social structure was: king/chief, warriors, druids (priests), brehons (lawmakers), bards, farmers, craftsmen, labourers and (k) _____.

The words 'Celt' and 'Celtic' are usually pronounced with a 'k' but the Scottish football club Celtic prefers the 's' sound.

connection   based   tribes   evidence   France
spoken   seen   oral   speak   slaves   name

3. THE GOLDEN AGE: CHRISTIANITY

Saint Patrick

The Romans left England around 400 A.D., because the Roman Empire was in decline. Then there were no soldiers to protect the towns. Irish raiders went to Britain to steal cattle, tools and weapons, and to capture slaves. On one of these raids a boy named Patrick was captured. He was forced to work as a shepherd on a mountain in county Antrim. After six years he escaped in a ship that was transporting Irish wolfhounds. Back home he believed he heard the voices of the Irish calling him back to convert them to Christianity. He became a bishop (in Auxerre, it is believed) and returned to Ireland in 432 A.D.

Converting the pagans

The Irish worshipped the sun and other gods, and the druids did not like to lose their high position, but Patrick worked hard to convert them. Leaders like King Laoghaire of Tara Hill [map] allowed him to preach. People say he used the shamrock to explain the Holy Trinity. People also say he drove all the snakes out of Ireland. He made Armagh [map] the centre of the Church in Ireland and was very successful in converting the Irish. But you can still see the pagan influence in Irish Christianity. For example, the Celtic festival of Halloween (hallow = holy, 'een = evening) used to be called *Samhain* ('end of summer'). On this day children wore disguises so that the spirits who came to take them could not recognize them; they also went door-to-door collecting treats, which at that time would have been fruit and nuts.

Monasteries

From around 500 A.D. many monasteries were founded, often in isolated areas where the monks could devote their lives to God. The most isolated monastery was on a small rocky island called Skellig Michael [map] off the coast of Kerry. In the picture you can see the 'beehive' cells the monks used to live in.

Skellig Michael, looking out to Little Skellig

Other monasteries were not so isolated and became great centres of learning, attracting thousands of students from Ireland and abroad. The larger monasteries also became hives of activity for farming and industry. They were the only Irish 'towns' at this time. In Glendalough, County Wicklow, there are some remaining parts of St. Kevin's Monastery, now a popular tourist site (*Gleann – dá – lough* is Irish for 'Valley – two – lakes').

Some monks spent their lives making beautiful copies of the Bible (the New Testament, in Latin). The Book of Kells, on view in Trinity College Dublin, is a famous example of their work. It is famous for its interlacing ('Celtic') designs and curious use of animals.

In Scotland, the monastery of Iona, founded by St. Columcille, is still in operation and is a popular pilgrimage centre.

Other monks travelled throughout continental Europe founding more monasteries, for example St. Fergal to Salzburg, St. Gallen to St. Gall, St. Kilian to Wurzburg and the most famous, St. Columbanus, to Gaul (France) and northern Italy.

A saint holding a monster's tongue. Image from the Book of Kells.

Glendalough Monastery, founded by St. Kevin in the 6th century

The word 'Propter' (= 'for') in the Book of Kells. Note the dots around some letters and animals.

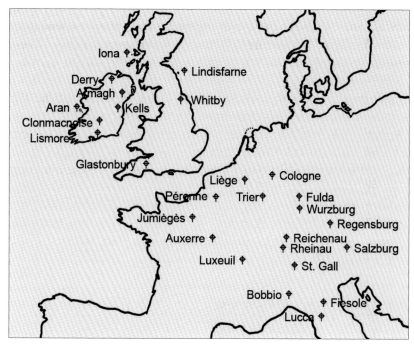

Irish Christian centres in Europe, 6th – 8th century

Tasks (ch 3)

1. Match the numbers with the letters:

1. Young Patrick looked after these.	a) a slave
2. This plant is similar to, but larger than shamrock.	b) preach
3. The female equivalent of a monk.	c) sheep and pigs
4. He works hard but gets no pay.	d) snakes
5. A change of faith.	e) a conversion
6. A monk's (and a prisoner's) room.	f) a nun
7. Home for the bee.	g) pagans
8. Sun-worshippers, for example.	h) clover
9. In Ireland, you'll only see these at the zoo.	i) a hive
10. To spread the word.	j) a cell

2. Mark the following true (T), false (F) or doubtful (D).

1. St. Patrick drove the snakes out of Ireland. ☐

2. He used the shamrock to explain the Holy Trinity. ☐

3. His burial place is believed to be in Downpatrick in Northern Ireland. ☐

4. He wore a bishop's mitre [= *hat* – see picture]. ☐

5. The first St. Patrick's Day parade was held in Dublin. ☐

6. In the Belfast parade in 1999 a 'Titanic' float actually crashed. ☐

7. On St. Patrick's Day in 1960 several pubs in Cork ran out of beer. ☐

8. The river Liffey in Dublin is dyed green on St. Patrick's Day. ☐

9. Green beer is served in many pubs in Ireland on St. Patrick's Day. ☐

10. The Leaning Tower of Pisa is lit up in green on St. Patrick's Day. ☐

11. Victoria Falls in Zimbabwe is lit up in green on St. Patrick's Day. ☐

12. The White House fountain flows green on St. Patrick's Day. ☐

An American greeting card

Statue of St. Kilian in Wurzburg, Germany. St. Kilian also worked in Austria.

Kate Middleton, the Duchess of Cambridge, presents shamrock to the Irish Guards (British army) on St. Patrick's Day 2018. The Irish wolfhound is the Guards' mascot.

3. Fill in the blanks:

Pilgrimages

In medieval times pilgrimages were very popular throughout Europe. In Ireland, two remain extremely popular with young and (a) _____ alike. These are at Croagh Patrick [map] and Lough Derg. Croagh Patrick is a mountain in Mayo (b) _____ it is believed St. Patrick spent the 40 days of Lent in 441. The mountain was probably a pagan shrine before St. Patrick changed it to a Christian (c) _____ .

Lough Derg is an island on a lake in Donegal. In (d) _____ places some people walk (e) _____ their bare feet. In Lough Derg you can only have tea and toast (f) _____ 36 hours. And you are not (g) _____ to sleep! It's a very demanding pilgrimage but those who make it usually return the next year for more of the (h) _____!

Climbing Croagh Patrick

Cross of the Scriptures, Monasterboice. Broken round tower in the background.

Pilgrims praying at the water's edge, Lough Derg

4. THE VIKINGS

The Vikings came from Norway, Sweden and Denmark. They were farmers and fishermen, but life for them was difficult when the land was hard and the sea was rough. In the 8th century they began to leave their own lands and travel in search of new places to trade with, to plunder and to live in. By this time many of the Irish monasteries had become wealthy centres of farming, trade and manufacture, besides education and prayer.

In 795 and again in 802 and 806 the Vikings attacked the monastery of Iona. The survivors fled to Ireland, where they built a new monastery in Kells [map]. All round the Irish coast monasteries were plundered: gold was stolen and valuable books damaged or destroyed (the Vikings were pagans and illiterate so they were not interested in the books themselves, just the decorated covers).

The Vikings were expert sailors, and their boats could not only sail around the coast but also up rivers, enabling them to reach the monasteries. Many monasteries had a round tower, which acted as a

Round tower in Ireland
Peace Park, Belgium

lookout tower or belfry or place of refuge. The door was built high so that it could only be reached by ladder. When the Vikings came some of the monks would take their valuables to the tower.

The Vikings did some good for Ireland. In 841 they built a town at the mouth of the river Liffey, at a part called Duib-linn, which means 'black pool' (you can see the dark water under Dublin Castle). Other towns like Cork [map], Limerick [map], Waterford [map] and Wexford [map] were also founded by Vikings and these ports became centres of trade and power.

Battle of Clontarf

The Vikings were successful in Ireland because the Irish leaders were always fighting among themselves. It was only when Brian Boru became High King in 1002 that a strong army was gathered. In 1014, at the Battle of Clontarf [map], he drove out the warring Vikings. He also had to defeat the King of Leinster who supported the Vikings! Brian was killed in his tent near the battle by a fleeing Viking. Many peaceful Vikings remained and adopted Irish customs.

Task (ch 4)

Fill in the blanks with the words and correct numbers (measurement and year) below. There are two wrong numbers.

Famous chalices

In the National Museum in Dublin you can see some beautiful gold and silver objects that the Vikings did not get their (a) _____ on. The Ardagh Chalice is one of (b) _____. It is made of over two hundred and fifty components. (c) _____ main materials are silver, gold and bronze. On it, if you (d) _____ closely, you can see designs of animals, snakes and human heads. And if you look (e) _____ closely you can make (f) _____ the names of the apostles! The Ardagh Chalice is 17.8cm high. It was found in a (g) _____ field in Ardagh, near Limerick, in 1868.

(h) _____ chalice found recently, the Derrynaflan Chalice, is 1.4cm higher than the Ardagh chalice, which makes it (i) _____cm in height. The Derrynaflan chalice was found in Tipperary in (j) _____, that's 112 years after the finding of the Ardagh Chalice.

more   potato   Its   those   out   look   hands   Another
20.2cm   19.2cm   1980   1970

Ardagh Chalice

Derrynaflan Chalice

5. CHE NORMANS

The Vikings were very successful in the North of France. They were called Normans (Northmen) and took over an area later called Normandy. Within two generations they had adopted the language, religion and customs of their French neighbours. Many Normans attacked parts of Spain, Turkey and Sicily and in 1066 they conquered England. For the next 200 years the official language of England was French.

Norman knight effigy, Thomastown, Co. Kilkenny

Invited to Ireland

In 1166 Dermot MacMurrough was King of Leinster (see map on next page). O'Rourke of Breffni did not like him because Dermot had carried off his wife. O'Rourke, with help from O'Connor, the king of Connaught, marched into Leinster to attack Dermot but Dermot fled to look for help. He went to Henry II of England who told him to ask for Richard de Clare, nicknamed 'Strongbow', the leader of the Norman army in Wales. Dermot did a deal with Strongbow: Strongbow could marry his daughter Aoife and succeed him as King of Leinster if he drove O'Rourke out.

Strongbow first sent over small armies but then came himself in 1170. He captured Waterford and then married Aoife (you can see a picture of the wedding in the National Gallery, Dublin). Dermot died in

Viking Reginald's Tower, Waterford. Strongbow and Aoife's wedding was celebrated here.

the following year and Strongbow became King of Leinster.

The Normans were expert soldiers and they built castles to hold their land. The Normans took control of Dublin, although their headquarters were at Trim Castle, about 40 miles away [map]. They then tried to take over Ireland, but they did not succeed, mainly because they did not come to Ireland in sufficient numbers. Another reason is that many of them began to speak Irish, adopt Irish customs and intermarry. In fact, they became 'more Irish than the Irish themselves'.

The main 'kingdoms' in Ireland, c. 1100

Trim Castle, Co. Meath, was built by the Norman lord Hugh de Lacy, who had married the daughter of Rory O'Connor. King Henry needn't have worried about this connection to the rebel, for de Lacy was decapitated by one of his advisors during the building of the castle.

Henry II, 'Lord of Ireland'

King Henry II, afraid that the Normans might become independent, came to Ireland (with 400 ships) in October 1171. He made himself 'Lord of Ireland' with the approval of Pope Adrian IV, the only English pope. Most of the Irish leaders submitted to him. Only the High King, Rory O'Connor, and the northern kings refused to submit. Henry gave a lot of Irish land to his barons.

Before returning to England, Henry received communion in Christ Church Cathedral in Dublin, his first communion since the murder of Thomas à Beckett in the previous December.

For some time the English kings were too busy fighting in France or Britain to pay much attention to Ireland, and they allowed Anglo-Norman leaders to rule as governers. These included the famous Fitzgeralds in Kildare and Butlers in Kilkenny [map], most of whom were speaking Irish (or Latin) and following Irish customs.

In a parliament meeting in Kilkenny in 1366 the *Statutes of Kilkenny* were agreed: settlers were forbidden to speak Irish, marry Irish people or adopt Irish customs. But it was too late: most of the native Irish and the Norman settlers were united in their opposition to English influence in Ireland. The only place where English rule was obeyed was in an area about 50km^2 around Dublin, called 'The Pale'.

Some Gaelic leaders like the O'Connors in Connaught and the O'Neills in Ulster continued fighting the Normans. They were sometimes loyal to the King, sometimes not, depending on when it suited them. Life continued like this for some time, with Irish leaders often fighting each other for control of territory, carrying out cattle raids etc, but they were generally 'loyal' to England as long as England did not interfere. They spoke Irish, followed Irish laws and customs, and paid little tax to the King.

Henry II reigned from 1154 to 1189. He was born in Le Mans, France.

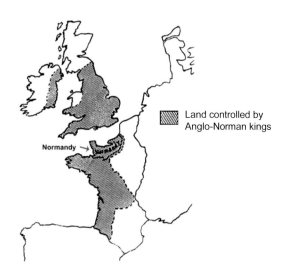

Normandy →

Land controlled by Anglo-Norman kings

Detail from the Bayeux Tapestry, 70 metres long, which depicts the Norman invasion of England, led by William the Conqueror, at the Battle of Hastings

Tasks (ch 5)

1. Rearrange the letters of the following words to find out where in Dublin Strongbow's tomb is: THISCR HHRCCU DECHALART

2. Fill in the blanks with the words below the text:

One of the reasons why the Normans were successful is that they built strong castles made of (a) _____. At first, though, they built (b) _____ towers on an artificial mound, or 'motte', with a wall, or 'bailey' round the foot of the mound. The later castles typically (c) _____ of a tower and the (d) _____ wall. Good (e) _____ of Norman castles can be seen at Trim, Ferns and Carrickfergus.

    For the next few (f) _____ Norman-Irish lords and their descendants ruled over large areas of land, using Irish and English law. They spoke Irish and English and (g) _____ Irish music. Only the (j) _____ around Dublin, known as 'The Pale' was controlled by the King.

    Irish musicians and storytellers became highly (h) _____, and the lords would look after them very well. If they didn't, the storytellers would tell a story or recite a poem criticizing them for being (i) _____.

centuries   wooden   surrounding   stone   stingy
respected   consisted   examples   enjoyed   area

Motte and bailey

VOCABULARY REVIEW, CHAPTERS 1–5 (blockbusters game)

If you are reading this on your own just go to the next page and see how many questions you can answer. If you can organise a quizmaster (e.g. teacher) and two teams (or two players) here are the instructions for the quizmaster:

Teacher puts the diagram below (without arrowed lines or words) on the board. One team tries to connect the squares across, the other vertically. Connections can be diagonal or zig-zag or straight. Toss a coin to see who will call out the first letter (any letter). The quizmaster will read out the question for that letter (questions on next page). Whoever, from either team, puts their hand up first (to avoid shouting) gives the answer. (Alternatively one team can be allowed time to answer before passing the question over to the opposing team.)

If the answer is correct the square is marked with horizontal or vertical lines as appropriate and the person who answered correctly chooses the next letter. All are eligible again. If the answer is wrong the opposing team gets the opportunity to answer. If nobody has the answer, clues should be given (the next letter in the word, the page number). In the example below, the up-down team has won.

Example:

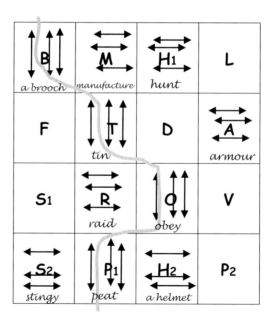

(After a player gives the right word the teacher writes it under the letter for consolidation. After a team has won, the leftover questions can be called and the answerers' initials put on the won squares.)

QUESTIONS FOR VOCABULARY REVIEW, CHAPTERS 1-5

The number after each question refers to the page on which the word first appears. The word may occasionally have a different form.

B What B is a piece of jewellery that you pin onto your clothes? 10
M What M means to make something, usually as an industry? 18
H1 What H means to try to catch or kill a wild animal? 7
L This L is the time when Christians fast before Easter. 17

F What F is a building for defence? 9
T Many food containers are made from this metal. 9
D You use this D to change the colour of clothes or hair. 16
A This A was seldom worn by the Celts. What is it? 11

S1 What S means wet land? 7
R If you do this R you attack a place and steal things. 13
O This O means to do what someone tells you. 21
V What V is the opposite of defeat? 11

S2 If you are this you don't like spending money. 23
P1 This P means bog material, sometimes called 'turf'. 8
H2 This H is worn to protect your head. What is it? 10
P2 This P believes in many gods, as the Romans did. 13

6. HENRY VIII

Henry Tudor came to the throne in 1509. He was married to Catherine of Aragon but wanted a divorce. The Pope did not allow it so in 1531 Henry established himself as leader of the (Protestant) Church of England and got a divorce. In 1533 he married Anne Boleyn and they had a daughter, Elizabeth. Anne was accused of adultery and was beheaded in 1536. Henry's other wives were: Jane Seymour (died 1537), Anne of Cleeves (married and divorced 1537),  Catherine Howard (beheaded 1542) and Catherine Parr (survived Henry).

For Henry, loyalty to Rome was disloyalty to England. He demanded that his subjects convert to the Anglican Church. He took land and monasteries from Catholic bishops and priests. Many were executed.

The end of the Fitzgeralds

At this time in Ireland Garret Óg Fitzgerald was the strongest Anglo-Norman leader and did not pay much respect to England. In 1534 Henry summoned him to England and had him put in the Tower of London. Garret's Son, Silken Thomas, then organized a rebellion against the King. The King's new deputy, Sir William Skeffington, with 2,300 men put down the rebellion. When everyone in the Fitzgerald Castle in Kildare surrendered they were all executed. The next time the Irish Parliament met, all the members voted to obey Henry and recognize him as head of the state church. Also, from this time the Viceroy (king's deputy) would always be an Englishman and there would always be English soldiers based in Dublin (until 1922).

In 1541 Henry was declared King of Ireland by the Irish parliament. Henry demanded that everyone in Ireland should become Protestant and follow English laws and customs. The Irish resisted change and they associated the executions and harsh treatment with the King's religion and English rule.

Henry gave land to Protestants, and the original Catholic owners had to rent it from their new landlords. From now on Protestants would have the upper hand in Ireland.

A good night's sleep

Henry VIII always travelled with his locksmith and a huge lock, because he was afraid of being assassinated in bed. Once the lock was fitted to the door of his bedroom Henry would sleep with the key under his pillow.

Tasks (ch 6)

1. Fill in the blanks:

Before Henry most English kings (a) _____ been content to let the Anglo-Norman lords govern with some independence. They knew it would be too costly (b) _____ try to control all of Ireland, especially as they needed their armies (c) _____ home and in France.

Henry, and his daughter Elizabeth after him, (d) _____ change all this and make Ireland the first English colony.

(e) _____ the desire to have colonies, done so successfully by the Spanish, they felt it was necessary to prevent Spain or any other enemy of England (f) _____ moving into Ireland, as this would probably be the end of England.

The execution of the Fitzgerald supporters was the first time that an English leader had been (g) _____ ruthless – Silken Thomas had been expecting to bargain for a little more independence – and it was the start of a long resentment of English rule in Ireland. Henry would (h) _____ preferred more negotiation and less bloodshed, but his and Elizabeth's representatives in Ireland believed mass executions were the best form of persuasion. Perhaps with less bloodshed Henry would have (i) _____ more success and Ireland would have united (j) _____ England more readily. Ironically, some of the strongest voices (k) _____ Henry came from monks brought to Ireland by the Normans: Franciscans, Dominicans and later Jesuits.

2. Write in once, when *or* whenever *in the sentences below.*

a) I'm very nervous. _____ the bell rings it makes me jump.

b) The students are usually quiet for the whole hour, but _____ the bell rings they jump up and start shouting.

c) _____ the bell rang for assembly this morning all the teachers were absent!

7. THE SPANISH ARMADA

The San Martín, the flagship of the Spanish Armada, captained by the commander-in-chief, the Duke of Medina Sidonia.

The Duke never wanted the command of the Armada, telling King Philip that he suffered from seasickness, but Philip insisted.

The ship carried 48 guns on two enclosed decks. It returned home safely but with some damage.

In 1588 Spain was the strongest country in Europe. King Philip II of Spain sent a fleet of 130 large ships with 30,000 men to invade England (*Armada* is Spanish for 'fleet of military ships'). First they anchored in Calais. Francis Drake sent fire ships towards them. The Spanish panicked; about 100 ships cut the ropes of their anchors to get away fast. Then the Spanish met a fleet of 197 English ships in the English Channel.

The English ships were smaller and able to attack and move faster. The Spanish ships couldn't turn back so they had to sail around Scotland and northern Ireland to return home. Medina Sidonia ordered: *"Be careful not to fall upon the island of Ireland for fear of the harm that may happen unto you upon that coast."** Due to storms, incorrect maps and having no anchors many were shipwrecked on the Scottish and Irish coasts. Only about half of the original fleet returned home to Spain. No English ships were lost.

Most of the sailors who landed on the west coast of Ireland were killed on the spot under English orders, or at least were beaten and had their gold and clothes robbed by the local people. Those who landed in the north of Ireland were luckier, though; some of the chieftains there were against England and did not kill them.

All around the north and west of Ireland there are places with names such as Spanish Port (Antrim), Spanish Rock (Donegal and Sligo), Spanish Arch (Galway) and Spanish Point (Clare) which remind people of the tragedy.

*Simplified from "Take heed lest you fall upon...".

"Spaniards drowned: 5,600. Spaniards slain: 1,100."
(Report of an English official on the losses in Ireland.)

Approximately 25 Spanish ships were lost off the Irish coast. Most of the sailors had drowned or died of sickness before having the chance to make it to shore. On one beach in Sligo 1,000 dead bodies were reported. English orders were: anyone helping the Spaniards would be killed. Dreadful stories of man's inhumanity to man remain:

> The Governor of Ireland, William Fitzwilliam, and the Governer of Connaught, Sir Richard Bingham, executed many hundreds of Spaniards, mainly tired and sick sailors, in Galway and Sligo. Don Luis de Cordova was spared when a large ransom was paid by his relatives in Spain.

> One of the ships, *La Trinidad Valencera*, was shipwrecked at Kinnagoe Bay [map]. About 500 men led by Don Alonso de Luzon reached land safely. Sir Hugh O'Donnell, a northern chieftain who was friendly with England, promised to help them but instead he had them killed. 300 were stripped naked and massacred, 150 escaped. The escapees and other Spaniards on the run were helped by bishops and other chieftains like O'Neill, McDonnell and MacSweeney.

> O'Donnell's son, Red Hugh O'Donnell, was in prison in Dublin and Sir Hugh wanted to show loyalty to England in order to have his son released. He marched to Dublin Castle with 45 Spaniards, 5 of which died on the way. His son was not released. O'Neill was angry with him for not helping the Spaniards. Soon after, O'Donnell retired to a prayer house. Don Alonso was released after payment of a ransom.

Francisco de Cuellar had some lucky escapes:

> The *San Juan de Sicilia* was shipwrecked on the Sligo coast. Hundreds of Spaniards drowned or were killed on the strand. Captain Francisco de Cuellar got to the strand by holding on to a piece of wood (he couldn't swim!). Then he started walking. He was robbed and beaten up twice. He was captured by a blacksmith who made him work as a slave. Then he was rescued and looked after by Brian O'Rourke of Breffni. He and eight other Spaniards then went to MacClancy, another chieftain. They defended MacClancy's castle against an attack by the Sheriff of Sligo, and MacClancy offered his sister in marriage as thanks. Cuellar politely refused and travelled on to the Bishop of Derry, who helped him and 10 other Spaniards to sail to Scotland. Eventually, Cuellar returned home, but was attacked on the way by a Dutch ship and was shipwrecked again, this time on the French coast! Once more he had to walk naked into a town (Dunkirk) looking for help.

English 'race' ship introduced at the time of the Armada

The wrecking of a Spanish Galleon off Port na Spanaigh, Antrim. John Carey. © Mrs. Jane M. Carey 2008.

Task (ch 7) — *Fill in the blanks, using the words below.*

A recipe for disaster – why the Armada failed

1. King Philip was not a (a) _____ expert, yet he gave many orders from his palace and didn't ask his commanders for advice.
2. The Duke of Parma, the leader of the Spanish forces in the Netherlands, was jealous of Medina Sidonia and didn't (b) _____ with him.
3. The Spanish Galleons were wide, and (c) _____ in the water, making them difficult to manoeuvre. The British ships were smaller, faster and more manoeuvrable, especially the new 'race' ships, 25 of (d) _____ were used.
4. Many Spanish ships were carrying (e) _____ canons and ammunition for when they landed, making them (f) _____ heavier.
5. Spanish ships had sea captains and army captains. This complicated the commands. English ships (g) _____ had sea captains.
6. The iron in the Spanish canon balls was brittle, with the result that many of the balls broke on impact, so they did (h) _____ damage than the English canon balls.

extra   which   military   cooperate   high   just   even   less

Bronze and iron swivel gun from La Trinidad Valencera (Ulster Museum, Belfast).
It was called 'the murderer' by the men using it because it would swivel back and injure them.

8. ELIZABETH INCREASES HER CONTROL OF IRELAND

Elizabeth I, Queen of England and Ireland from 1558 to 1603, wanted to protect her country from the Spanish. She was afraid that the Spanish King would use Ireland as a 'back door' into England, so she decided to strengthen her control of Ireland.

Religion and power were combined in Europe at this time, and many Protestants and Catholics were killed. The Queen of England was (and the UK Monarch still is) the head of the Church of England, the largest Protestant church in England. A number of Catholic bishops and priests were hanged in England and Ireland for not recognizing the Queen as head of the Church. Irish land was mapped and regional leaders (chieftains) were obliged to obey the Queen's deputy in Dublin and follow English laws. If they did this, the Queen gave them the title 'Earl'.

Most of the leaders became Earls but they did not all obey the Queen. In the north especially, the O'Neills and the O'Donnells decided to keep their independence. Hugh O'Neill defeated a large English army in the Battle of the Yellow Ford [map] in 1598, which made Elizabeth very angry. Among his officers was Pedro Blanco, a survivor of the Armada.

Assistance from Italy and Spain – the Smerwick massacre

In September 1580 about 700 Italians and Spaniards (mostly Italians) were sent by the Pope and King Philip of Spain to help in the Munster rebellion. Commanded by Sebastiano di San Giuseppi of Bologna, they landed near Dingle [map] and stayed in Smerwick Fort. According to one report, about 100 of the Italians had to be sent back home due to illness, as they were not used to the damp and cold of the Irish autumn.

No help came from the Desmond clan in Munster, most of whom were weak and hungry from years of fighting. Lord Grey, the Queen's deputy in Ireland, arrived at the fort with 4,000 men. The Italians, Spanish and Irish held out a white flag of surrender. Lord Grey spoke with them, and then had them all killed.

To understand such cruel treatment, it may be helpful to remember that in France in 1572 over 10,000 Protestants (Huguenots) were killed by Catholics.

More assistance from Spain; the Battle of Kinsale 1601

In September 1601 a fleet of 24 ships with 3,500 Spanish troops led by Don Juan d'Aquila landed at Kinsale [map]. They expected help from the Desmond chieftains in Munster, but this help did not come because the Munster rebels had been defeated in previous years. In October Lord Mountjoy, the commander of the Queen's forces, marched from Dublin and surrounded the town.

O'Neill and O'Donnell were hundreds of miles away in the North. O'Neill knew that the Spanish had enough food and ammunition to last for some time.. He attacked some English-controlled towns near Dublin to make Mountjoy come back but Mountjoy stayed in Kinsale.

The Spanish defended well against Mountjoy, but by December their food was running low (also Mountjoy's). O'Neill and O'Donnell marched south to Kinsale. After the long and dangerous winter march their men were in poor condition, and standing around outside Kinsale in the rain for days did not improve matters. O'Neill wanted to wait longer and starve Mountjoy out, but O'Donnell and the Spanish were impatient. Finally the rebels, with 6,500 men, fought against Mountjoy's 7,500 on Christmas Eve. The battle lasted only one hour.

The Irish made running attacks in disorder but Mountjoy's footmen and cavalry used good strategies. There was also poor communication with the Spanish – although they had held parts of the town very bravely early on, they did not know when to join in the main battle.

Plaque unveiled in Simancas Castle in 1991 by Don Hugo O'Donnell, a descendant of the Earl

The rebels were defeated. 1,200 Irish were killed, English losses numbered 12. Most of the Spaniards were allowed to return home. Some of the rebels were allowed to go to Spain with them.

Hugh O'Neill returned to Ulster. Hugh O'Donnell went to Spain to ask for more help, but he died there a year later. Some historians say he was poisoned by an English spy. He was given a state funeral, his hearse passing by the King's palace in Valladolid.

The Flight of the Earls

It was expensive for Elizabeth to have a large army fighting in Ireland, so she allowed Hugh O'Neill to keep his land in Ulster, but he had to sign a treaty in 1603 with Lord Mountjoy. According to this treaty he would obey and enforce English law and encourage his people to observe English customs, wear English dress, etc.

O'Neill knew, however, that the government in Dublin did not trust him. Most of the English and Anglo-Irish were angry that he had not been punished, and they wanted to take his land. Year by year the pressure built up. In 1607, fearing an assassination or attack from Dublin, Hugh O'Neill, Rory O'Donnell and other leaders sailed to Europe with their families in a French ship. This is known as the 'Flight of the Earls', and marks the end of Gaelic independence in Ireland.

Pope Paul V greets O'Neill at the Quirinale Palace in Rome

Tasks (ch 8)

1. Fill in the blanks with the words below each section.

'The O'Neill'

The O'Neill clan of Tyrone had been one of the strongest in Ireland since the 5th (a) _____. Hugh was elected 'The O'Neill', the leader of the clan, around 1594, in the traditional way at Tara.

   Hugh was (b) _____ up as a nobleman, receiving part of his education in England. He was (c) _____ with English ways and was generally loyal to the Queen. However, after the rebel chieftans of Munster were killed and their lands given to English settlers, O'Neill (d) _____ to become a rebel also. He imported lead from England to make bullets (he said it was to repair the roof of his castle). He was a thorn in the side of the Queen, defeating her armies and (e) _____ her much money, but after Kinsale his position became weak and he decided to leave Ireland for Spain to ask King Philip III for help. However, (f) _____ to bad weather the ship had to land in France. Philip did not want O'Neill to come to Spain, and told him to go to Rome.

decided   century   costing   familiar   due   brought

Arrival in Rome

Philip and some cardinals arranged a grand (g) _____ for O'Neill and his family into Rome (10 coaches with 6 horses each) where he was greeted by the Pope. Philip continued to support O'Neill in Rome but did not (h) _____ him to come to Spain. Philip had started peace negotiations with England, and he kept O'Neill as a (i) _____ against England, to strengthen his hand in the negotiations. O'Neill, on the other (j) _____, constantly wrote letters to Philip asking him for support to go back to Ireland with Spanish troops.

   O'Neill died in 1616 and was (k) _____ in the church of San Pietro in Montorio, beside his brother-in-law Rory O'Donnell.

   King Philip also paid for the funeral of O'Neill's wife in Rome. She was his fourth wife. He had (l) _____ twice. His second wife died young. His third wife ran away because he was unfaithful.

   When the chieftains left Ulster their land was taken by the government and (m) _____ among Protestant settlers from Scotland and England.

threat   distributed   entrance   divorced   hand   allow   buried

2. Look at the examples of conditional sentences:

Past (3rd conditional):

If O'Neill had won at Kinsale, he would* have become leader of Ireland.

Past-to-present (3rd to 2nd conditional):

If O'Neill had won at Kinsale, Northern Ireland might* now be part of the Republic of Ireland.

*Would or might, sometimes could, are possible here.

Now fill in the blanks:

a) If King Philip _____ known more about the English ships, he _____ _____ built faster ships.

b) If the Earls _____ remained in Ulster, the plantation _____ _____ been much smaller.

c) If Henry _____ _____ insisted on getting a divorce, the Church of England _____ _____ now be in existence.

d) If King Philip _____ helped O'Neill, Ireland _____ now ___ a part of Spain.

e) If the plantation had been smaller, … [Finish this sentence yourself.]

Church of St. Pietro in Montorio, Rome, resting place of Earls Rory O'Donnell and Hugh O'Neill

9. PLANTATION

The only way that England could keep control of Ireland was to 'plant' the land with English farmers and landlords. This was first done in Munster in the 1550s. Over 120,000 hectares of land was given to Englishmen who were loyal to the crown. One of these was Sir Walter Raleigh, a favourite of Queen Elizabeth. He was the first man in Ireland to smoke tobacco, and the first to plant potatoes (do you know why it was he?). He developed the timber industry, exporting wood to France and Spain, mainly for making barrels. As more and more wood was exported for making barrels and ships, within a century Ireland became one of the most treeless countries in Europe.

Sir Walter Raleigh & son

The Irish who were thrown off their land fought back with some success, but after the 'Flight of the Earls' there were no chieftains to lead them.

The Plantation of Ulster (1609 - 1650)
In the north, the lands of the O'Neills and the O'Donnells and anyone who had helped them were confiscated and distributed among Scottish and English settlers. Most of the Scottish planters were Presbyterians. Presbyterians do not agree with the Church of England system (they elect their leaders democratically and don't have bishops), but these were generally loyal to England and built good farms and villages.

Rebellion and Cromwell
In 1641 there was a rebellion. Many of the planters and their families were killed by Catholics who had been removed from their land. Many others, fearing for their safety, emigrated to America. There was an attempt to unite the 'Old English' (Catholics from the Norman times) with the native Irish but this failed.

Cromwell, an English military man who had defeated the English King Charles I to get control of the parliament in London, came to Ireland in 1649 to restore order. His Irish enemies included royalist supporters because Charles I was tolerant of Catholics. Cromwell first headed for Drogheda, [map] which refused to surrender. As an example to other towns and 'as a righteous judgement of God' he massacred all its inhabitants. Wexford suffered a similar fate, then most other towns surrendered. Again, land was taken from the Catholics and this time it was used to pay Cromwell's officers. Those who had owned the land were forced to go to Connaught, a province in the west of Ireland, which has poorer land (farm labourers were allowed to stay, to work for their new landlords). 34,000 royalist soldiers went into exile. 10,000 more were transported to the West Indies to work as unpaid servants. The Caribbean Island of Montserrat is the only non-Irish country to have a national holiday on St. Patrick's Day.

Task (ch 9)

Fill in the blanks with the words below.

The plantation was not (a) _____ successful. The planters found that they needed to keep Irish workers and tenants, so not all the native Irish went to (b) _____ as ordered. Also, many soldiers sold their land and (c) _____ to England. Other soldiers who remained married Irish Catholic girls and (d) _____ up their children as Catholics. However, by the end of the 18th century (e) _____ land in Ulster was in Protestant hands. Incidentally, in 1613 the city of Derry (f) _____ its name to Londonderry to show its (g) _____ to the London businessmen who developed it.

changed   brought   most   entirely   gratitude   Connaught   returned

Ulster: shaded counties are those planted after the 'Flight of the Earls'. Land in Antrim and Down was sold privately to Scottish settlers, not distributed by the government.

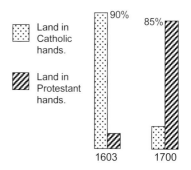

Changes in the ownership of Irish land in the 17th century

The sketch above is of the altar area of Ballintubber Abbey in Mayo (founded in 1216) some time after its burning by Cromwell's soldiers. Despite Henry VIII's laws and the fact that for years it had no roof or floor the Abbey never stopped being used as a place of worship by the local people. Below is a recently taken photograph.

10. THE PIRATE QUEEN

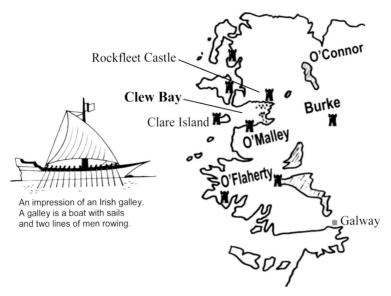

Rockfleet Castle

O'Connor

Clew Bay

Burke

Clare Island

O'Malley

O'Flaherty

Galway

An impression of an Irish galley. A galley is a boat with sails and two lines of men rowing.

Clew Bay, clans and some castles

Grace O'Malley is her name in English, but most people know her as *Granuaile*, pronounced Grawñe Wale. She came to be leader of the O'Malley clan, who controlled the seas around Clew Bay, and owned a lot of the land there too. No other Irish clan controlled the seas like the O'Malleys. Clew Bay was easy to defend, with over 100 islands (365 at low tide). The O'Malleys' main castle was on Clare Island.

Grace was born in 1530, and by this time the O'Malley clan, and the neighbouring O'Flaherty clan, had been strong for 300 years. During the Norman expansion both clans sided with the Normans and did not help other Connaught clans such as the O'Connors who were fighting against the Normans. Remember that in these times it was almost 'every clan for itself'; there was little concept of a unified nation, even a unified province. Galway had a sign over one of its gates which expressed the fears of its citizens: *"Good Lord, deliver us from the ferocious O'Flahertys"*. Galway followed the English laws and demanded taxes for exporting goods. The O'Malleys ignored these laws.

The O'Malley chiefs made money by collecting taxes from fishing boats, mainly English, French and Spanish, that fished off the O'Malley coasts. And like other clans the O'Malleys would have carried out raids, stealing cattle etc. Unlike other clans though, they would have carried out their raids by sea, attacking coastal towns. They also sailed to Portugal and Spain, trading fish and cattle hides for wine and other goods. Scotland was another trading destination. But the seas were dangerous: navigational instruments were very basic and there were many pirates ready to attack.

As a child Grace was a typical 'tomboy': she did not play with dolls or other girls' toys. Instead she wanted to work on her father's boats. She also loved to play cards with the sailors – and often won! When her father refused to allow her onto his galley because she was a girl she cut her hair and dressed as a boy.

Better than her husbands

When she was 16 Grace married Donal O'Flaherty, son of the chieftain of the clan in Connemara. It should have been a good match, bringing the two clans closer together, but Donal was a troublemaker and he caused problems with other clans.

Donal was killed by one of his enemies in 1572. Grace and her three children returned to the O'Malley lands. Grace had to defend her castles from enemies, Irish and English. She also worked hard on the sea, escorting foreign ships or pirating from them. Once, when her galley was being attacked by north African pirates she became annoyed with her crew because she had to show them how to shoot a musket.

Grace married Richard 'Iron' Burke of the rebel Burke clan and lived in Rockfleet Castle. Richard was restless and fought against other clans, trying to increase his power, but this attracted the attention of the Governer of Connaught. In 1574 the Governer sent an English army by sea from Galway to attack Rockfleet, but Grace won the battle. Richard was away fighting other clans as usual.

In the meantime the Lord Deputy Sir Henry Sydney was forcing all chieftains to submit to English law and pay rent to the Queen. Grace's father Owen agreed, but died soon after in 1574. Grace took the initiative and went to the Lord Deputy who was in Galway at the time. Sydney's report says: *"She offered the services of three galleys and 200 fighting men in Ireland or Scotland. She is a notorious woman in all the coasts of Ireland."*

Queen Elizabeth ordered Sydney to allow Grace to keep her property and galleys (she had about 8) even though her loyalty to England was questionable. Elizabeth did not want expensive battles.

A ruthless new governer

Things got bad for Grace when a new Governor of Connaught was appointed. Sir Richard Bingham believed that the only way to stop rebels was to hang them or put them in prison. He held meetings with clan members. He told them they had to obey and to enforce English laws and to pay taxes. At one meeting he hanged 70 people. Some historians believe that if he and other English leaders had allowed the chieftains more time to change from the Irish laws there would not have been so much rebellion.

Rockfleet Castle, a typical tower house of a rich Irish family

Bingham confiscated Grace's herd of cattle, numbering over 1,000, because she had helped the Burke clan in their defence against him. Bingham hanged the ninety-year-old Burke chieftain. Then Bingham went to Grace's son Owen and also took his cattle, then hanged Owen and 18 of his soldiers. Grace was imprisoned in Limerick, then in Dublin Castle, but after a year and a half she negotiated her release.

Grace sailed up to the O'Neills and the O'Donnells in the north for safety. She heard about the future Spanish invasion but did not promise to take part. However, she would transport soldiers from Scotland and around Ireland for the chieftains. During this time her second husband died, making her a widow again.

A meeting with the Queen of England

After three months Grace returned to Mayo. Gradually Bingham got control of Clew Bay. Grace, seeing that now she had neither cattle nor ships, decided that there was only one way to secure her future. She took her greatest gamble and wrote to Queen Elizabeth. In her letter she explained that she had no widow's property and that she should be allowed to continue to attack the Queen's enemy ships along the coast (O'Neill had used the same excuse for his fighting: that he was fighting the Queen's enemies). In July 1593 the Queen's secretary replied with eighteen questions about Grace's family and her possessions. Elizabeth must have been curious about this woman who commanded ships with fighting men in a time when women generally were subservient to men.

Yet again, Bingham moved against Grace and arrested her son Tibbot-na-Long ('Tibbot of the ships'). Bingham had also imprisoned Grace's brother Donal-na-Piopa ('Donal of the pipes') some months before that. Grace decided to sail to London immediately.

Luckily, Grace, accompanied by an O'Flaherty, got to England safely and sailed up the Thames without any problem. The leader of the strongest country in the world and the leader of a clan of pirates met in Greenwich Castle, the Queen's summer residence. It must have been a strange sight: one queen with powdered face and wearing a wig, jewels and a richly embroidered gown; the other queen wearing a long plain cloak and speaking in Latin because her English was not so good.

The meeting was successful for Grace. Elizabeth wrote to Bingham instructing him to release the brother and son of the 'aged woman' and to allow some of their tax money to go to Grace. Bingham was angry but eventually released the two men. However it is not clear if Grace's son or brother looked after her as well as they should have.

Grace died around 1603 in Rockfleet Castle. She would have heard about the defeat of her friends the O'Neills and O'Donnells at Kinsale. She may have even helped them in their march to Kinsale, but would not have fought with them. Grace was a rebel at heart but she knew that it was useless for loosely organized clans to resist a unified and powerful enemy.

Tasks (ch 10)

1. Fill in the blanks. Some initial letters of the missing words are given.

Once, when Grace was (a) re_____ from a sailing trip via Dublin she stopped at Howth Castle to (b) p___ a visit. She was told that the family were at dinner and they did not want to be (c) d_____. The gates were closed (d) ag_____ her. Grace was so angry that she (e) kid_____ the Baron's son. Only when the Baron (f) apo_____ did she give back his son. Grace also made the Baron (g) p_____ to keep an extra place at his dinner table for any (h) unex_____ guest in the future. This custom is still being (i) f_____ today.

▲ Howth Castle

◄ An impression of the meeting between Grace and Queen Elizabeth

2. Modal perfect:

She _must have_ done it = I'm 95% sure that she did it.
She _can't have_ done it = I'm 95% sure that she didn't do it.
She _might have_ done it = it is a possibility (in the past).
She _should have_ done it = this was the right thing to do but she didn't do it.

Use a modal perfect in the remarks below, following the example.

0. A: Grace cut her hair in order to get on her father's boat.
    B: *She must have been a real tomboy.*

1. A: Why didn't Grace stay with O'Neill in the north?
    B: *I don't know. She _____ _____ wanted to check up on her castles, or maybe she just got homesick.*

2. A: Grace's first husband was a troublemaker.
    B: *Yes. She _____ _____ divorced him as soon as possible.*

3. A: The Governer of Connaught hanged a ninety-year-old man.
    B: *Yes. He _____ not _____ been so cruel.*

4. A: One of Grace's sons, Murrough, actually joined with the Governer.
    B: *Really? He _____ _____ been a very loving son!*

5. A: Elizabeth asked 18 questions.
    B: *Wow! She _____ _____ been very curious!*

6. A: Elizabeth told Bingham to help Grace.
    B: *Yes, Elizabeth _____ _____ liked her.*

7. A: Why was the Governer so cruel?
    B: *I don't know. He _____ _____ had a bad childhood.*

QUESTIONS FOR VOCABULARY REVIEW, CHAPTERS 6-10

If you are working alone just see how many questions below you can answer.

Otherwise, teacher/quizmaster please copy the table on page 24, putting in the letters below. Then follow the instructions.

The number after each question refers to the page on which the word first appears in these chapters. The word may occasionally have a different form.

S1 This S means to give up, stop fighting and lose. 26
P A king's house, for example. 30
E1 If you have to live outside your country you are in this. 37
C1 What C is a narrow sea between two countries? 28

N1 This N means to have no clothes on. 29
A This A is necessary for guns. 30
N2 This N means to talk business, to try to get a good deal. 41
U If you are not true to your spouse you are this. 34

C2 This C is a big coat with just one button and no sleeves. 42
S2 This S is a person who is still alive after an accident or battle. 31
H1 This H is the car that carries your coffin. 33
I This I means, "Don't pay attention." 39

E2 It's easy to make a law, but sometimes difficult to E it. 33
T1 This T means wood, especially the wood business. 36
H2 This H means the skin of an animal. 40
T2 If you annoy someone greatly, you are a T in their side. 34

11. KINGS IN CONFLICT

King James II

William of Orange

The Last Catholic King of England

In 1685 James II, son of Charles I, became King of England. He had converted to Catholicism in France in 1669. James appointed Catholics into positions of power, making himself unpopular with the establishment. Protestant leaders did not want a Catholic ruler, so they invited James' Dutch son-in-law, Prince William of Orange, to come and take his place.

William came with 14,500 soldiers and 3,750 horses in 500 ships. James first went to France for help, then to Ireland with French money, arms and men. The Catholics in Ireland hoped that James would restore their land, but James was mainly interested in getting back his crown.

The Siege of Derry

James marched to the north and approached the city of Derry. The people inside did not know whether to let him in or not. As he was about to enter, a group of apprentice boys shut the city gate. James besieged the city for 105 days, closing off the river. The city walls were strong, but the people inside became so hungry that they had to eat candles, cats and rats. In the end, ships from England broke through the boom [barrier] across the river and brought supplies in. James had to give up the siege.

Every year the Shutting of the Gates (12 August) and the Relief of Derry (2 December) are commemorated with parades and the burning of an effigy of 'Lundy the Traitor' (Lundy was appointed Governor of Derry by William, but was prepared to surrender the city to James).

Apprentice Boys Parade

Effigy of Lundy

The Battle of the Boyne [map]

In 1690 William, made King of England by the parliament, came over to Ireland. The two kings met at the river Boyne, about three miles from Drogheda, James with 25,000 men and William with 36,000. James was a poor leader and fled when the fighting became tough. James' army was defeated. James was given the nickname 'James the shit' by the Irish who observed his flight.

'King Billy' on his white horse. Mural in Belfast.

James went to France, where he died in 1701. While there, many of his Irish soldiers (then called 'Wild Geese') joined him to fight in France. He arranged for King Louis to pay them the French wages, which were less than the English ones – he was obviously very stingy!

Ian Paisley (left) First Minister of Northern Ireland presents Bertie Aherne, Prime Minister of the Republic, with a gun used in the Battle of the Boyne at a ceremony at the battle site in 2007

Tasks (ch 11)

1. Fill in the blanks, using the words below.

The Siege of Limerick

After the Battle of the Boyne the last (a) _____ to hold out against William was Limerick. The (b) _____ of the Irish there was Patrick Sarsfield. He managed to destroy a lot of William's heavy guns and (c) _____ outside the city. Once when a hole was made in the city wall, women joined in the (d) _____ by throwing bottles and stones at William's army. The siege was stopped for winter. William went back to England leaving his Dutch General, Ginkel, in charge.

A French ship arrived with General St. Ruth and some (e) _____ but no troops. In the following year Athlone was (f) _____ and the French general was killed in the battle. Louis XIV wanted Sarsfield to continue fighting and promised to send more troops but Sarsfield did not believe him and decided to (g) _____.

On 3 October 1691 the Treaty of Limerick was (h) _____. This promised religious tolerance, and it (i) _____ the Irish soldiers to go abroad, where they fought well, mainly in the French and Austrian armies, winning many honours. These soldiers, numbering over 10,000, became (j) _____ as the 'Wild Geese'.

known   place   signed   defence   leader   ammunition
allowed   captured   supplies   surrender

Holding the wall at Limerick

The Treaty Stone, Limerick, where the treaty was signed

2. Read this text, and page 45, and answer the questions below.

The Dutch connection

There is a hill town in the south-east of France originally named after a Celtic god Arausio. Over time the name *Arausio* changed to *Aurenja* and finally *Orange*. There is no connection with the fruit.

From 1530 the town and county were owned by a rich German family, the House of Nassau. William I, Prince of Orange and Nassau (1533-1584) converted from Lutheranism (German Protestant) to Catholicism in order to keep ownership of Orange and to be friendly with the Emperor of France and King Philip of Spain. After this he was made Governer of the northern part of The Netherlands, which was mostly Calvinist (Dutch Protestant). The Calvinists protested about the Inquisition and Philip II sent thousands of Spanish soldiers to stop them. This Spanish occupation lasted 80 years. William I joined the Calvinists and helped them when he heard about Philip's plans to kill them.

William II, Prince of Orange and Nassau (1626-1650), married Mary Stuart, the eldest daughter of Charles I, king of England.

William III, Prince of Orange and Nassau, was born in 1650, a few days after the death of his father. In 1677 he married 15-year-old Mary Stuart II, daughter of James who became King of England in 1685.

When Parliament made William king in 1689 they also enacted *The Bill of Rights,* which stated that in future the Monarch could not cancel a law made by parliament. Also according to the Bill of Rights, a non-Protestant or a Protestant married to a non-Protestant could not become Monarch.

After defeating James, William and Mary spent the rest of their lives as King and Queen of England (and Scotland and Ireland).

William died in 1702 in London. His horse tripped on a mole-hill and threw him to the ground. He died from his injuries.

The present monarchs of The Netherlands still have the title 'of Orange and Nassau'. The flag of William was orange, white and blue. The Netherlands flag was later changed to red, white and blue. An orange ribbon may be attached to the flag for royal ceremonies.

a) What relation was William III's father to James II?
b) William III was related to James II in two ways. What were they?

The Orange Society and 'The Twelfth'

The Orange Order was founded in Co. Armagh in 1795 for people who supported British rule and Protestantism. The members are called 'Orangemen'. They celebrate the anniversary of the Battle of the Boyne every year on 12 July (a national holiday in Northern Ireland). They march/parade through the streets with banners and flags to the sounds of bands with lambeg drums. They then usually finish with a picnic and speeches about following the Bible rather than the Pope, and loyalty to the Crown. At night bonfires are lit, some with the tricolour on top.

About 2,000 Orange parades take place throughout summer in Northern Ireland. There are Orange parades also in Glasgow, Toronto and Adelaide.

Orangemen marching, playing the fife and lambeg drum. The drum is very loud and very big. Its diameter is 0.9 metres, its depth/width is 0.65 metres, and its weight is 16.7 kilos.
The wearing of a bowler hat in the parades is an old tradition.

Tasks (ch 11 contd.)

3. Match the numbers with the letters:

1. an organization of religious people	a) convert
2. disagreement, fighting	b) commemorate
3. change your religion	c) tolerate
4. make it as it was before	d) an order
5. when witches were burnt	e) a trip
6. a learner of a trade (e.g. carpentry)	f) conflict
7. a journey to a place, and return	g) the Inquisition
8. put up with	h) restore
9. remember in a special way	i) supplies
10. usually delivered by truck	j) an apprentice

12. THE PENAL LAWS 1559-1829

The Irish parliament in Dublin was composed entirely of Church of Ireland (a branch of the Church of England) Protestants, and, not surprisingly, these wanted to keep control. They did not agree with the Treaty of Limerick. Catholics, Presbyterians and others, who made up 80% of the population, were excluded from law-making.

In the 1690's a number of laws were passed to ensure the dominance of the Church of Ireland members. The list below includes some which had already been in existence.

1. Catholics were forbidden to own arms.
2. Catholics could not buy land.
3. When a Catholic died, his land was to be divided among his sons. If the eldest son became a Protestant he would get all the property.
4. Catholic bishops were banished.
5. Catholic children could not be sent abroad to be educated.
6. Catholics were forbidden to run schools.
7. Catholics were not allowed to hold a position in the civil service.
8. Catholics were not allowed to become officers in the army or navy.
9. Catholics were not allowed to enter the legal profession.
10. Catholics were not allowed to enter parliament.
11. A Catholic could not own a horse worth more than £5.

The Penal Laws were successful in depriving Catholics of political and financial power. However, many of these laws were not enforced. After a number of years the authorities often turned a blind eye whenever a new Catholic church or school was built.

However, a good Catholic education in Ireland was almost impossible and throughout the 17th century many Irish Colleges were set up in European cities: Paris, Louvain, Rome, Salamanca, Lisbon, Prague…

In 1795 the government supported the building of Maynooth College in Ireland for the education of Irish priests, to reduce the influence of revolutionary ideas learnt on the Continent.

Hedge schools

Most Catholics did not like the schools built by the government because they were Protestant and taught British culture. Many Catholic teachers organized 'hedge schools', which were schools under trees/hedges or in barns, and parents paid them to teach Irish history and culture, also

Catholicism, and of course Latin, an important language at that time.

In 1832 the government started building schools suitable for Catholics.

Mass rocks

Most Catholic priests were allowed to celebrate mass as long as they obeyed the laws of the crown, but some priests were rebellious and so they were not approved by the government. There were few churches, so many masses were said on rocks in fields, away from the road where soldiers might be passing. These fields are still called 'mass rock fields'.

Mass rock in Wexford. Commemorative masses are still said at some mass rocks in Ireland.

Task (ch 12)

Fill in the blanks, using the words below.

The Irish Parliament

(a) _____ the Penal Laws there were other laws which caused animosity in Ireland. These were trade laws (b) _____ by the English government. In 1699 the English parliament passed an act (c) _____ the export of woollen goods from Ireland. The Irish parliament was (d) _____ to the English parliament. Many people complained about this. One of (e) _____ was Jonathan Swift, Dean of St. Patrick's Cathedral (Protestant) in Dublin and (f) _____ of *Gulliver's Travels*.

The American War of Independence (g) _____ Irish politicians to think of self-government. In 1782 Henry Grattan, Prime Minister of Ireland, repealed many of the laws which discriminated (h) _____ Catholics and Presbyterians. The future looked (i) _____ for people of those religions.

author   these   Besides   against   made
prohibiting   brighter   subordinate   encouraged

13. THE FRENCH IN IRELAND

In 1789 the Bastille (royal prison in Paris) was stormed by a crowd of French people. All over Europe there was a lot of interest in the struggle of the French for 'liberty, equality and fraternity'. Theobald Wolfe Tone, a young Protestant lawyer from Dublin, wanted to unite all Irishmen to fight for an independent Irish Parliament. Presbyterians did not have full religious and political freedom. They agreed with Wolfe Tone and joined together in Belfast to form the Society of United Irishmen. There were thus two groups of people opposing the British government: the Ulster Presbyterians and the southern Catholics.

Attempted invasion at Bantry Bay

Wolfe Tone went to France for help. The French were at war with Britain and were keen to export their revolutionary ideas. In 1796 15,000 French troops under General Hoche sailed from Brest for Ireland. Due to bad weather only half of the fleet reached Bantry Bay [map]. These still could not land there and turned back. The British and Irish governments were alarmed. A search for arms was ordered, houses were burned and suspects were flogged, mainly by Irish militia.

The Wexford rebellion

In 1798 there was a rebellion in Co. Wexford which was successful for some time. Shamefully, a mob of Catholics got out of control and killed a large number of innocent Protestants. Reinforcements soon arrived from England. The rebels, armed with pikes and farm tools, and led by a priest, Father Murphy, were defeated at Vinegar Hill [map]. Many of the rebels were executed; others were transported to Australia.

Battle in Wexford. The rebels use pikes against the cavalry.

Fr. Murphy statue in Tullow

Father Murphy was tortured, hanged and decapitated in Tullow **[map]**, Co. Carlow. His head was put on a spike as a warning to others.

Killala Bay

Having sailed from La Rochelle, 1,000 French soldiers under General Humbert landed at Killala Bay **[map]** in Sligo on 22nd August 1798. About 2,500 Irishmen joined them and they defeated a government army at Castlebar. Humbert needed more Irish support but he did not get it. His Irish soldiers were mostly farmers and not well organized. They probably felt that there would be no point in fighting against the larger government armies. On 8 September 20,000 trained British soldiers from Dublin arrived at Ballinamuck. There was a short battle but soon Humbert surrendered. The French were treated as prisoners of war; hundreds of the Irish were butchered.

Half-hanging, one form of torture used on the rebels

Statue of pikeman in Ballinamuck

"*After several unsuccessful attempts, behold at last Frenchmen arrived amongst you...*

"*Union, Liberty, the Irish Republic! Such is our shout. Let us march. Our hearts are devoted to you.*"

From General Humbert's proclamation in Killala. Humbert was shocked to find that hostility between Catholics and Protestants played such a part in this rebellion, unlike the French one.

Lough Swilly

In October another French force of 3,000 troops in 10 ships, with Wolfe Tone, tried to land at Lough Swilly [map] in Donegal but it was defeated by the British navy before it could do so. Wolfe Tone was arrested. He refused to be hanged as a criminal and demanded to be shot by firing squad as a French soldier. His demand was refused and he cut his throat in prison.

The end of the Irish Parliament

In 1801 the members of the Irish Parliament voted to end it (getting a payment in return) and move all power to the parliament in London. The old parliament building is now a branch of the Bank of Ireland, and the House of Lords room inside is open to the public.

Wolfe Tone in French army uniform, as he was when he was captured

La Hoche, the leading French ship, damaged, being towed by HMS Doris in Lough Swilly

A rebel song/poem

Oh, the French are on the sea,
    Says the <u>sean-bhean bhocht</u>. →
The French are on the sea,
    Says the sean-bhean bhocht.
Oh, the French are in the bay,
They'll be here without delay,
And the Orange will decay,
    Says the sean-bhean bhocht.

Irish *sean-bhean bhocht* = 'poor old woman', pronounced shan van vocht.
    Old and young women were metaphors for 'Ireland' in rebel songs.

Tasks (ch 13)

1. Can you work out the missing words in this verse?

Is a bhfaighimid fós ár saoirse? = And will ___ get _____ freedom?

  Ars an tSean-bhean bhocht. = Says the _____ ____ _____

Is a bhfaighimid fós ár saoirse?

  Ars an tSean-bhean bhocht.

Beimid saor 'dir bhun is craobh = We'll be _____ 'tween base (of tree) and _____

Beimid saor ó thaobh go taobh = _____ ___ _____ from side to _____

Saor go deo le cabhair na naomh = _____ forever _____ the help ___ ____ saints

  Ars an tSean-bhean bhocht.

2. Fill in the blanks. Some initial letters of the missing words are given.

Another Protestant Irish hero

Robert Emmet wanted another insurrection. After his expulsion
(a) f____ Trinity College he went to France, (b) w ___ he tried to
interest Napoleon in his ideas. Napoleon was busy preparing to make
(c) h_____ Emperor. Emmet returned to Ireland and using his
(d) o___ money he bought arms and planned an uprising. His attempt to
take Dublin Castle in 1803 failed and he (e) h___ in a house in
Rathfarnham, a suburb of Dublin. The police located him and found
letters in his pocket (f) add_____ to his girlfriend, Sarah Curran.
They contained some of his (g) pl_____. He was (h) h_____, drawn
and quartered outside St. Catherine's Church in Thomas Street, and his
head was (i) disp_____ to the crowd.

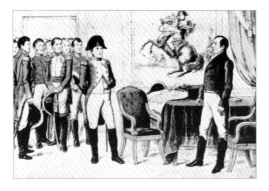

Robert Emmet with Napoleon
in Paris.

Emmet's speech in court in
Dublin became famous, and
Abraham Lincoln studied it before
making his Gettysburg Address.

Martello towers

The British feared an invasion from Napoleon. Indeed, Napoleon had prepared 25,000 troops and established the *Légion irlandaise* for an invasion of Ireland but this never happened. From 1804 Martello towers were built around the coasts of Ireland and England. These are strong circular towers with walls 2.5 metres thick and a canon on top. The design is based on a tower in Mortella Point in Corsica.

There are about 35 Martello towers still standing in Ireland, some in poor condition, some converted to houses or shops. The most famous one is the James Joyce Tower in Dun Laoghaire, Co. Dublin, which was converted into a museum to commemorate the writer.

Martello Tower at Seapoint, south Dublin, converted into offices.
A shelter has been added for bathers.

The James Joyce Museum in Dun Laoghaire. In 1904 Joyce spent a few days here with some friends, including Oliver St. John Gogarty. He set the first chapter of *Ulysses* in the tower, making it a 'must visit' for Bloomsday fans.

Badge of the Irish Regiment, *'la Légion irlandaise'*, established by Napoleon in 1803.

The men never fought in Ireland but did in Spain, Netherlands and Poland, suffering great losses. The regiment was dissolved in 1815, by which time the proportion of Irishmen in it was 10%.

14. DANIEL O'CONNELL

In 1801 the Act of Union was passed and Ireland was then governed from Westminster. Some penal laws still existed, for instance Catholics could not sit in parliament, they could not be judges, and they could not have a high position in the civil service.

Most Catholics were poor country people (peasants) and would never think of a job in politics or the civil service, but they felt that their situation might improve if they had emancipation.

Daniel O'Connell, the son of a wealthy Catholic landlord, was born in County Kerry [map]. He studied law in France, then later in London and Dublin. As a barrister, he became interested in Catholic emancipation.

No violence

O'Connell decided that he would not use violence to win emancipation, for three reasons: 1) while he was in France he saw the bloodshed in the French Revolution and this affected him greatly; 2) he killed a man in a duel (with pistols) in Dublin, which he regretted very much; 3) he saw how violence had failed with Emmet and Wolfe Tone before him.

In 1823 O'Connell, with the help of thousands of volunteers, formed the Catholic Association. The membership subscription for the association was only one penny per month, so almost all the Catholics in the country could join. Now the Catholics became confident, having an organization which would fight for their rights.

In 1828 O'Connell won a famous election in County Clare [map] to be an MP (Member of Parliament) in Westminster, although, as he was a Catholic, he could not take his seat. His following was so strong, however, that the English government had to give in and allow emancipation for the Catholics. The 'Catholic Relief Act' was signed into law in 1829. O'Connell could now sit in Parliament.

The Duke of Wellington was born in Co. Meath and spent his early childhood in Dublin (where now is the Merrion Hotel, opposite Government Buildings). He was a well-off Protestant, but as army commander in Spain he ordered his soldiers to respect Catholic priests and churches. He refused to damage Paris after his victory against

Napoleon at Waterloo. He became Prime Minister of Britain and Ireland in 1828. Fearing insurrection in Ireland, he persuaded King George IV to sign the Catholic Relief Act. The King hated doing so, and the Duke's conservative party was weakened by divisions within.

Task (ch 14)

Fill in the blanks with the phrasal verbs below.

The decline of O'Connell

After his success in winning emancipation, O'Connell (a) _____ _____ to break the Act of Union, which did not allow a parliament for Ireland. He organized 'monster meetings' at which hundreds of thousands of people would (b) _____ _____. The most famous of these was at Tara, the ancient meeting place of chieftains. O'Connell believed that the English government would again (c) _____ _____ when they saw such support, but things didn't (d) _____ _____ that way. The government banned a meeting planned in 1843 to be held at the site of the Battle of Clontarf. O'Connell, not wanting bloodshed, obeyed the ban and (e) _____ _____ the meeting. Even so, he was jailed for three months. From then on he became politically weaker, and others had to (f) _____ _____ the fight, such as Thomas Davis, a Protestant lawyer.

   O'Connell became ill and died in Genoa in 1847 on his way to Rome. His heart was sent to Rome and his corpse to Dublin, as he had asked. A round tower was (g) _____ ___ over his tomb in Glasnevin cemetery.

give in - turn out - set out - turn up - called off - put up - carry on

Crowds cheer O'Connell on his release from prison

Statue in O'Connell St., Dublin

15. THE GREAT FAMINE

In 1841 the population of Ireland was 8.1 million. The main cause of the population growth was that when a farmer's son married he got a part of the land, so there were many early marriages. While landlords became rich, spending most of their time in Dublin or London, many Irish families became poor, with just a little land to grow potatoes on. Grain was also grown, but this was for export. The potato was the staple diet in Ireland – in fact for about three million people it was their only food.

In September 1845 in the south-east of Ireland people found that their potatoes were rotting in the ground. Potato blight had struck. Soon the blight affected more than half the country and there was little to eat. Indian corn (a type of maize) was imported and sold cheaply. The corn was also used as wages for working on new roads and other work 'invented' for the poor. Unfortunately, however, the government at that time in Westminster believed in a *laissez-faire* (non-interference) approach to economics; state charity was not a priority. Workhouses (up to 130) had been built since 1838, where poor people could live and work and get some food. These were terrible places, all overcrowded, the 'last resort', where families were separated (different rooms for adult males and females and children). Workhouses had also been built in England for unemployed people.

No free food

In 1846 there was blight again, but this time it affected the whole country, and the winter was the coldest in memory. Fishermen had sold their nets in order to buy food, thinking that the famine would not continue, but it did. Still the government in London remained short-sighted and would not intervene with direct help. Charles Trevelyan, Assistant Secretary of the Treasury, organized more relief work (mainly the building of roads) but he felt that the famine was a punishment from God for lazy people. Starving people searched for food everywhere, eating seaweed and anything they could get their hands on.

Eventually, in 1847 the government set up 'soup kitchens', places where free soup was distributed. This still wasn't enough, however, as in the winter of that year people were dying of starvation and sickness.

Even in the workhouses 2,000 people were dying every week. There was no blight in 1847, but most of the seed potatoes had been eaten, so crops were few and small. While grain was still being exported, Indian corn was being imported for the workhouses. Every week, hundreds of ships from America, England, Spain, Italy and France were delivering food into Cork and Westport. British and Irish Quakers helped fishermen to buy back their nets and farmers to sow different crops.

Eviction & emigration

Tenants who could not pay their rent were evicted and their houses destroyed. Between 1849 and 1854, 49,000 families were evicted. In Clare in 1848 1,000 families were evicted in six months. Not all landlords were cruel – some were kind, and some also became bankrupt as no rent was being collected.

To escape from the nightmare many people had to emigrate, mainly to Liverpool and America. Thousands never arrived at their destination as they were so weak and ill, and the ships were overcrowded and filthy.

About a million people died in the Great Famine. And something else started dying too – the Irish language, for the emigrants and their families saw the value in learning English to get a job abroad.

Emigration continued for many years, even up to the 1990s, because Ireland was a poor country. Ireland's most famous emigrant was Annie Moore, the first person to pass through the Ellis Island Immigration Station in New York, on 1st January 1892.

The number of people in the world who claim to have Irish ancestry is 80 million.

Emigrants waiting to board a ship. In 1847 about 20,000 Irish arrived in Liverpool every month.

Statue of Annie Moore and her brothers in Cobh, Cork

1. *Read the clues below and guess the words. To help you, all the words end in either* -tion, -ness *or* -ty. *Also, the first letter of each word is given.*

1. Another word for sickness.   i_____
2. The state of being poor.   p_____
3. The result of not eating.   s_____
4. Preparedness.   r_____
5. The end of the journey.   d_____
6. Group of people with a cause.   o_____
7. Moving to another country.   e_____
8. Division/spread/sharing.   d_____
9. Lack of attention to the future. s_____
10. For helping the poor.   c_____
11. Something instead of another.   s_____
12. An acute lack.   s_____
13. The noun form of 'homeless'.   h_____
14. The number of people.   p_____
15. Forced removal from home.   e_____

A family after being evicted from their home. The doorway has been boarded up. The house would later be destroyed by the landlord's men. The police would protect the landlord's men.
Eviction was encouraged by the government as a way to make larger, more efficient farms. Evicted families usually ended up in workhouses, and landlords were told to pay for their ship tickets to the US and Canada.

*2. Change the sentences from Active to Passive, following the example.
It is not necessary to write the 'by…' part (the agent).*

> *Example:*
> A: The landlords evicted the tenants.
> P: The tenants <u>were evicted</u> *(by the landlords).*

1. A: The government imported Indian corn.

   P: Indian corn …………………………..………… .

2. A: The government set up soup kitchens.

   P: Soup kitchens ……………………………...…… .

3. A: The government had built workhouses.

   P: …………………………………………...…… .

4. A: People also grew grain.

   P: …………………………………………...…… .

5. A: People were still exporting the cash crop.

   P: ……………………………...………………………..… .

6. A: People could say it.

   P: It ………………………….………………… .

7. A: The people had eaten most of the seed potatoes.

   P: …………………...…………………………………..……… .

8. A: Some landlords were not collecting any rent.

   P: No rent …………………………….………… .

9. A: The government has erected many Famine memorials.

   P: …………………………………………………...… .

Attitudes towards immigrants

Immigration into the US was made difficult by law, so most ships landed in Canada. Hospitals immediately became overcrowded; sheds were used to hold the thousands more who were sick and dying. John Mills, Mayor of Montreal, was kind, but he, like some priests and doctors, caught the disease and died.

Many moved to the US, avoiding border guards who tried to stop them. Complaints about immigrants bringing disease and cheap labour led to rioting against Irish Catholics in Boston and Philadelphia, where houses and a church were burned, and 13 people were killed. In spite of that, many Americans donated generously to the poor in Ireland.

One emigrant who made it to Detroit was John Ford, from Cork, whose wife died in Canada. His grandson was Henry Ford, founder of the modern automobile industry.

3. Fill in the blanks, using the words below.

Blight

Potato blight is a fungus, *phythophthora infestans,* which settles on the (a) _____ of the potato plant. It grows rapidly and (b) _____ hours it can destroy a whole field of potatoes. It needs moist, warm air to spread. The blight had been (c) _____ in America in 1843, and it (d) _____ to mainland Europe in June 1845. Thousands of people who (e) _____ on the crop died. There was a drought in Europe in 1846 which helped to kill the blight (f) _____. However, there was no drought in Ireland. Many attempts were (g) _____ to find a cause for the blight, but it wasn't (h) _____ 1882 that a Mr. Millardet in France discovered a treatment for it. Now 'blight warnings' are given on TV when the (i) _____ is suitable for the fungus to grow and spread, and farmers are advised to spray their (j) _____.

> seen   made   until   leaves   there   relied
> weather   within   spread   crops

4. Fill in the blanks. Some initial letters are given.

Choctaw Indians

In the winter of 1831, 21,000 Choctaw Indians were (a) <u>fo_____</u> to leave their ancestral homelands in Mississippi and move to Oklahoma. Almost half of the tribe died on the 500-mile (b) <u>j_____</u> , called the 'Trail of Tears'. Sixteen years (c) _____ a group of Choctaw heard of the famine in Ireland and decided to help. (d) <u>A_____</u> they were poor themselves the Choctaw raised $170 for Irish famine relief, a lot of money at that time, especially from people who had very (e) <u>l_____</u>.

Now every year a group of Irish and Choctaw meet in Ireland and America to do a sponsored walk for (m) <u>f_____</u> relief in Africa.

Gary White Deer, of the Choctaw Nation, visits the Skibbereen famine cemetery, Co. Cork, in 2009.

In 2018 Taoiseach Leo Varadkar went to the Choctaw Council in Oklahoma to announce a new scholarship for Choctaw people to study in Ireland

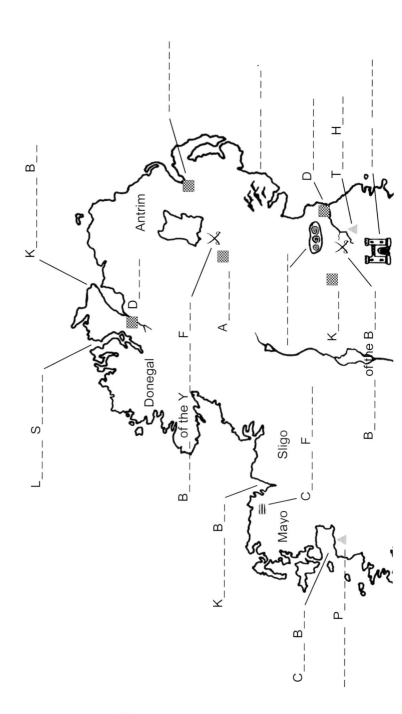

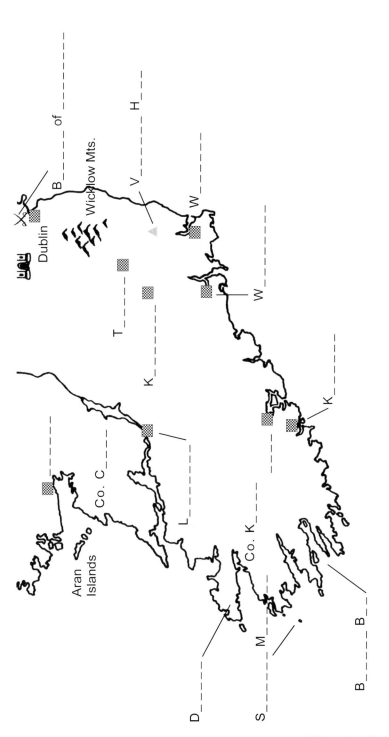

QUESTIONS FOR VOCABULARY REVIEW, CHAPTERS 11-15

If you are working alone just see how many questions below you can answer.

Otherwise, teacher/quizmaster please copy the table on page 24, putting in the letters below. Then follow the instructions.

The number after each question refers to the page on which the word first appears in these chapters. The word may occasionally have a different form.

V This is a person who offers to work for no money. 57
S1 Someone who did something wrong, the police think. 52
M This M lives in the ground and ruins your garden. 48
S2 This S is the general name for plants that grow in the sea. 59

T This T can mean a path, a track. 63
R When food or crops are old they do this. 59
F This F is a verb meaning to be afraid. 56
P To tell someone it's good to do something, to make them do it. 58

I The terrible time when 'witches' were burnt. 48
B1 If you B something you don't allow it to happen. 58
S3 This S means 'fight to get free'. 52
G Another word for cereals, e.g. wheat, corn, etc. 59

D When there is no rain we have this. 63
W This W is like a salary but you get paid every week. 46
B2 A house for animals or animal feed. Part of a farm. 50
S4 If you are a member of an association you must pay this. 57

16. THE FENIANS

Thomas Davis advocated the use of force to gain independence

Fenian banner

People like Thomas Davis became impatient with Daniel O'Connell's peaceful methods and formed the Young Ireland movement in the 1840's. Davis launched a new newspaper, *The Nation*, which encouraged people to think of being Irish and not just Protestant or Catholic or rich or poor. He wrote the popular ballad "A Nation Once Again". He died of a fever at the age of 31.

After the famine the Young Irelanders became more militant but their rebellions failed because of bad organization, spies and the poverty of the people. The leaders were transported to Australia or escaped to France and America. In America they set up the Fenian Brotherhood in 1858 (named after the *Fianna*, a legendary Irish warrior tribe). They then helped to set up a corresponding movement in Ireland called the Irish Republican Brotherhood (IRB), headed by James Stephens. The name Fenian became used for both groups. The aim of the movement was to ignore parliament and use force to make England grant independence to Ireland.

Experience in the American Civil War

By the 1860's many Irishmen had got experience fighting in the American Civil War. They had heard reports of the famine and some had personal experiences of the hard times. They blamed the famine on England and they came back to Ireland to fight in a rebellion. Irish soldiers in the English army were also recruited by Fenians. Important leaders included John Devoy, who had fought in the French Foreign Legion, and others who had fought in the Mexican-American war. The rising in 1867 in Cork, Waterford, Limerick and Dublin was a total failure due to informers (spies) and poor communication. A ship came from America with thousands of rifles but it arrived too late and had to turn back.

Meanwhile in England there was a lot of support for the Fenians among the working class Irish (Karl Marx and Friedrich Engels became very interested in the movement). Two members were rescued from a prison van in Manchester but a policeman got killed during the action. This caused the loss of popular support in England. Three leaders, none of whom had fired the shot, were hanged. This caused popular support for the Fenians to rise again. The song "God Save Ireland" was composed in their memory. Later, a bomb used in an attempted prison break-out killed several people nearby. Again support fell.

Fenians attack a prison van in Manchester

Some leaders in America became impatient and organized an attack on Canada but this, like so many attempts, was a failure, again mainly due to spies and poor organization.

The Catholic church was hostile towards the Fenians. The Pope condemned them and they were not allowed to attend church services. In reply, leaders like Charles Kickham told the church to keep out of politics.

Of political value

Although their actions were failures the Fenians became well known, and politicians began to pay heed to them. Irish MP's like Isaac Butt who wanted Home Rule were able to use the publicity to their advantage. Butt, and Karl Marx, called for an amnesty for the prisoners. In two years seven Fenians had died in English jails, and four had gone insane. One famous prisoner, O'Donovan Rossa, had spent 123 days on bread and water, 28 days in dark solitary confinement and 34 days with his hands handcuffed behind his back. He was released on condition that he would not return to Ireland. He went to America and continued to work for the organization there.

1. Put the lines of the songs in the correct order. The first line is correct.

A NATION ONCE AGAIN

a) *1* When boyhood's fire was in my blood
b) __ For Greece and Rome who bravely stood
c) __ Our people free of chains*
d) __ And then I prayed I yet might see
e) __ A nation once again!
f) __ I read of ancient freemen
g) __ Three hundred men and three men
h) __ And Ireland, long a province, be

*Altered from the original: *Our fetters rent in twain.*

GOD SAVE IRELAND

i) *1* God save Ireland, said the heroes
j) __ Oh, what matter when for Erin dear we fall.
k) __ Whether on the scaffold high
l) __ God save Ireland, said they all
m) __ Or the battlefield we die

2. Fill in the blanks, using the words below.

The Land League

Tenant farmers had few (a) _____ and could be evicted from their homes and (b) _____ off their land by greedy landlords. The landlords could also (c) _____ the rent at any time.

In 1879 the Land League was (d) _____ by a Fenian, Michael Davitt, to help tenant farmers fight (e) _____ high rents and evictions. Then he strengthened the Fenian movement by forming an (f) _____ between the farmers, the militant Fenians and the Irish Parliamentary Party. Davitt invited Charles Stewart Parnell, a landlord, to (g) _____ president of the Land League. Parnell held the three sections together with great (h) _____. Home Rule became a very hot (i) _____ in Westminster, and tenant farmers became strong in Ireland.

become   rights   founded   raise
alliance   thrown   topic   skill   against

17. PARNELL – 'THE UNCROWNED KING OF IRELAND'

*"We will never gain anything from England
unless we tread upon her toes."* (Parnell 1877)

Charles Stewart Parnell was born in Avondale, Co. Wicklow (now a public park) in 1846. His mother's father was 'Old Ironsides', an American naval commander in the Anglo-American war. His father, a liberal politician, died when Charles was 13. Charles was sent to schools in England, including Cambridge, where he didn't do very well, especially at writing and public speaking. Back in Ireland he decided to go into politics, partly because he didn't know what else to do, and partly because he believed in the importance of land reform (helping tenant farmers). Other Anglo-Irish (Protestant) families called him a traitor because working for land reform meant working for the Catholics. His decision did seem ironic because he was a Protestant landlord, though not a rich one. Parnell also believed in the importance of Home Rule: a parliament for Ireland. He was elected as an MP for the Irish Parliamentary Party. At first, because he was a bad speaker nobody paid him any attention, but gradually he improved and his support grew.

In 1876, the 100th anniversary of the American Declaration of Independence, Parnell visited the United States and made speeches about Irish independence. This built up his support there, and the donations he received helped with his finances.

To make the (British) Parliament take notice of the Irish Parliamentary Party, Parnell, Michael Davitt and others used 'obstruction' tactics: they talked endlessly during House of Commons debates – one debate lasted twenty-six hours. The result was that normal business was often disrupted, and Parnell became famous. Back in Dublin he received a standing ovation for ten minutes.

In 1879 Parnell became president of the Land League. This was an organization which aimed to give land back to tenant farmers and to prevent rent increases and evictions. The Land League did not agree to using force, but many frustrated farmers and Fenians used extreme violence, even murder. Parnell was against violence but didn't break his connection with the Fenians. He advised people to have nothing to do with landlords or any tenants taking over an evicted farmer's land. The result was that many landlords were not served in shops and were generally ignored. The first landlord to be treated in this way was a Captain Boycott. The word 'boycott' then entered the English language.

Parnell went to America again and in two months visited sixty-two cities, including Washington. The Irish-Americans were generous with their donations. The Land League became very strong, its membership rising to 500,000.

Parnell strengthens the Irish Party

In 1880 Parnell became leader of the Irish Parliamentary Party. He unified the party and made each member swear to vote for the party's policies at all times. Since then most political parties have followed this example. The party became a force within the British Parliament. In 1881 Gladstone's government introduced a bill reducing rents by twenty percent and guaranteeing fair rents and fewer evictions. The bill was passed, but the militant half of the Land League insisted on more. Parnell stayed between the militants and constitutionalists. The Land League was declared illegal and Parnell was sent to Kilmainham Gaol (where he was given a comfortable room) for 7 months.

While he was in prison his sister Anna did a lot of work with the Ladies' Land League, helping poor and evicted families. When Parnell was released from prison he and Davitt preferred to work

Parnell being interviewed in Kilmainham Gaol

politically, and hardly acknowledged Anna's hard, practical work.

After the land reform Parnell and the Irish Party then pushed for Home Rule. Gladstone began to support Home Rule in order to stay in government with the votes of the Irish Party. However, things were made difficult by the American and English Fenians who wanted complete independence: they assassinated the Chief Secretary of Ireland in the Phoenix Park, then over the next few years they carried out bombings in English cities.

It took some time for things to calm down, and only by 1890 did Home Rule become a possibility with Gladstone again. But then, there was a scandal: Parnell was involved in a divorce case between Willie and Kitty O'Shea. Willie was a member of the Irish Party and Parnell had lived with Kitty for many years. Religious leaders in Britain and Ireland told the people not to vote for Parnell. He lost a lot of votes but refused to resign. This caused a bitter split in his party. He died a short time later in 1891 at the age of 46 from illness and overwork.

THE LOVE STORY OF PARNELL AND 'KITTY' O'SHEA

Parnell was a fighter. In school in England he fought against some of his English classmates there, and back home he would dominate his brother and sister. In politics very few people could win an argument with him, not even the Prime Minister, who eventually supported Home Rule. He was tall and handsome, but often became ill because he worked so hard.

Katharine Wood was born of an upper class family in England in 1845 and lived near London. Willie O'Shea was of a middle-class Irish Catholic family. His father, who was a solicitor in Dublin, bought him a captaincy in the English cavalry. Willie and Katharine first met at a party when she was 16. They continued to see each other but Katharine did not seem as much in love as Willie was.

Willie always lived beyond his means, including buying expensive bouquets for Katharine (and asking his father for the money). Katharine and Willie married in 1867. Willie was often away on business, usually unsuccessful business, and depended on Katharine's rich aunt to help him out. Katharine became bored with Victorian dinner-parties, often being left alone by Willie.

In 1880 Willie became an MP for Co. Clare. Katharine continued to help him, and invited important people to dinner. One of these was Parnell. Parnell didn't open his invitations so Katharine went to the House of Commons and personally gave him one:

He looked straight at me, smiling. He had curiously burning eyes. I had a sudden thought: "This man is wonderful!" A rose fell from my blouse. He picked it up, put it close to his lips and put it in his button-hole.

Years later I found that rose in an envelope with my name on it among his private papers. When he died I laid it upon his heart. *

Parnell came to dinner and very soon after that they started meeting secretly. When he was speaking in the House of Commons Katharine would go to listen to the debate in the public gallery, and Parnell would give her a secret message with his handkerchief. Parnell had to travel to Ireland regularly, and constantly wrote letters to Katharine.

When Parnell was in Kilmainham Gaol Katharine had his first baby, which died soon after birth. Willie thought it was his. Katharine disliked Willie, who was an egoist and often insulted his colleagues in the Irish Party. He and she had lived apart on-and-off since 1875, and Katharine only allowed him to come to her house by invitation. Willie must have suspected that his wife and Parnell were having an affair but said nothing, perhaps because he was waiting on Katharine's rich aunt to die and leave her her fortune. Parnell rented a house in Brighton and he and Katharine often went there.

Katharine's aunt died in 1889 and willed all her estate to Katharine, who had looked after her for many years. However, Katharine's siblings contested the will, so nothing would be decided for about three years. Willie became impatient and filed for divorce. Parnell's English political friends broke away from him because some English religious leaders were condemning him as an adulterer. When Parnell also lost support in his party and in the country towns of Ireland his dream of getting Home Rule died. Some of his enemies laughed at Katharine and blamed her for the crisis, using the name 'Kitty' (her short name was Katie, Parnell called her 'wifie' and 'queenie').

Parnell and Katharine got married in June 1891, soon after the divorce was settled. Parnell still travelled back and forth to Ireland, making speeches often in the rain, trying to recover his support, but his health deteriorated. He died in Katharine's arms in October of the same year.

Parnell was buried in Glasnevin Cemetery in Dublin. 250,000 mourners turned out for his funeral. However, no gravestone was put on his burial place until 1940, when a boulder was brought from his native Wicklow. Katharine died in 1921 and was buried near Brighton. Katharine had three children by Willie and three by Parnell. She never came to Ireland. There are over 100 Irish pubs named after her.

* *Charles Stewart Parnell: His Love Story and Political Life*, by Katharine Parnell. [Excerpt abridged.]

Tasks (ch 17)

1. Match the numbers with the letters.

1. A parliamentary discussion
2. A unified group of politicians.
3. A form of limited independence.
4. Forceful removal from your home.
5. Refusing to do business with someone.
6. A landlord receives rent from these people.
7. Parnell's relationship with Kitty O'Shea was/caused this.
8. A person elected to Parliament.
9. Before a law is made, this is what is debated.
10. When a political party is divided.

a) a scandal
b) tenants
c) a split
d) a member
e) a debate
f) a bill

g) eviction
h) boycotting
i) a party
j) Home Rule

2. Fill in the blanks. Some initial letters are given.

a) Parnell's maternal grandfather was in the American _____ .
b) At college, Parnell wasn't very good __ writing or public speaking.
c) "A Protestant landlord in favour of land being given to Catholic farmers? How i_____ ."
d) Parnell's long speeches caused <u>dis</u>_____ in the House of Commons.
e) Parnell's affair was <u>con</u>_____ by religious leaders.
f) Willie always lived beyond his _____ , spending more money than he earned.
g) Katharine was the main beneficiary of her aunt's _____ .
h) Katharine's brothers and sisters _____ the will.
i) Willie ran out of patience and f_____ for divorce.
j) Towards the end, Parnell's health _____ .

3. Answer the following questions.

a) How old was Parnell when he died?
b) How old was Katharine when she died?
c) How old was Katharine when she married Willie?
d) In what year did America declare independence?

18. THE GAELIC REVIVAL

As the power of the landlords was reduced and people had more of a say in local government, there was a degree of contentment in Irish life, especially in the countryside. Ireland was part of the British Empire, on which the sun never set. Home Rule was still on the agenda in Westminster, although unionists, especially those in the north, were against it.

Some people were afraid that Ireland would lose its cultural identity, so a number of organizations were set up.

Queen Victoria reviews her Dublin soldiers in the Phoenix Park. 1900

The GAA (Gaelic Athletic Association)

In 1884 soccer and rugby had become popular in Ireland, and Irish sports were dying out, so a group of men led by Michael Cusack decided to found an organization in 1884 to promote Irish games, especially hurling and Gaelic (Irish football). Hurling is probably the oldest ball-and-stick game in the world but at that time there were no written rules, consequently players often got injured.

The IRB (Fenians) infiltrated the organization and used it as a recruiting ground, but most members just wanted to play the 'new' sports. However, the rules were strict and until the 1970's members were banned from playing foreign sports. And not until 2006 were soccer or rugby allowed to be played in Croke Park, the GAA's and Ireland's largest stadium. The amateur rule has been maintained.

Today there are over 2,500 GAA clubs in Ireland, and Irish holidaymakers are recognizable by the sports jerseys they wear, bearing the name of their county (the inter-county championships are popular).

Hurling. One of the oldest and fastest ball-and-stick games in the world, revived by the GAA.

A form of hurling called camogie, played by girls, was started in 1904

The Gaelic League

After the famine the Irish language declined and now most schools taught through English. Only in the west did people still speak Irish. Douglas Hyde, a Protestant professor of languages, founded the Gaelic League in 1893. Its aims were to restore Irish as the main language of the country, and to promote Irish culture.

Douglas Hyde became the first President of Ireland in 1938

Irish was taught by travelling teachers, who now had the advantage of the newly-invented bicycle. A newspaper and books were published in Irish, and feiseanna (Irish culture festivals) and céilis (Irish dances) were held.

Many people were influenced by the Gaelic League, but some of these decided to use the promotion of Irish culture as a stepping stone towards violent rebellion. Douglas Hyde disagreed with this and resigned in 1915.

Pádraig Pearse became editor of the Gaelic League's newspaper. He set up a boy's school which gave priority to Irish cultural subjects. He gradually became convinced that a blood sacrifice would have to be made to gain independence:

> *"There's nothing but our own red blood*
> *Can make a right Rose Tree."*

Pádraig Pearse had an eye disfigurement, so he posed for photos with full profile

The Abbey Theatre

Anglo-Irish literature began to be promoted by new, mainly Protestant, writers. William Butler Yeats was the most famous of these, and he and two others founded a new theatre, the Abbey Theatre, in Dublin. Yeats encouraged playwrights to write plays about Irish topics. Many of the plays were patriotic and may have encouraged rebellion, although this was not Yeats's intention. Some plays became world famous, such as *The Playboy of the Western World* by J.M. Synge, and *Juno and the Paycock* by Sean O'Casey.

From a portrait of Yeats by Seán O'Sullivan in the Abbey Theatre

Task (ch 18)

Test your knowledge of Irish culture. Mark these true (T) or false (F).

1. The Irish language is an Indo-European language. ☐

2. The Irish language has a writing system which pre-dates Latin. ☐

3. In traditional Irish dancing the dancers may not swing their arms above shoulder height. ☐

4. Much Irish set dancing is danced to the polka rhythm. ☐

5. In Gaelic football the ball may not be thrown. ☐

6. In hurling you are not allowed to carry the ball on the stick. ☐

7. The most famous Irish legendary hero played hurling. ☐

8. Maeve, the Irish legendary queen, went to war over a bull. ☐

9. There was a riot in the Abbey Theatre when one of the actors said, "girls in their underwear". ☐

10. Sean-nós (old style) singing is only performed by men. ☐

11. The recipe for Guinness was invented in London. ☐

12. Uilleann pipes (elbow pipes) have a greater range of notes than the Scottish bagpipes. ☐

American girl taking part in a feis in San Diego. This may never have happened without the founding of the Gaelic League.

Freddi Tekook, an uilleann piper from Germany, joins in a trad session in Greystones, Wicklow

19. ᚈHE 1916 ᚱISING

Military organisations

In 1913 James Connolly formed the Irish Citizen Army in Dublin to protect men on strike from police brutality and to work towards a socialist republic.

Part of Connolly's army outside Liberty Hall

In the same year another nationalist force, the Irish Volunteers, was formed in Dublin in response to the Ulster Volunteers, who were against Home Rule. Many members of the IRB (Irish Republican Brotherhood, also called Fenians) joined the Irish Volunteers. Britain tolerated the formation of these armies, perhaps hoping they would never really fight, or at least that they would be ready to fight for England.

In 1914 World War 1 began. The British Government decided to postpone Home Rule for Ireland. The Irish Parliamentary Party encouraged Irishmen to join the British army and 200,000 did so, especially because many were poor and they would appreciate a soldier's pay. However, militant republicans were angry about the postponement of Home Rule and they decided it was time to fight for an independent Ireland. They said, "Britain's misfortune is our opportunity," and, "Burn everything British except their coal."

Arms in short supply

Many of the Irish Volunteers trained with hurleys due to the lack of guns. Eventually 1,500 rifles (old Mausers bought in Germany) were brought into Howth and Wicklow on sailing boats. Another attempt to import arms failed: a German ship, the Aud, loaded with rifles and machine guns was captured off the coast of Kerry and her captain scuttled her.

Guns delivered at Howth in the *Asgard*, with Molly Childers, wife of the boat's owner, and friend

Mainly Dublin

The Rising was first planned for Easter Sunday, then cancelled, then ordered for Easter Monday. In Limerick, Cork and other towns the orders were misunderstood, or due to the capture of the Aud the morale had gone low. So, only in Dublin was a serious attempt at insurrection made. On 24 April 1600 republicans, consisting of about 250 of James Connolly's men and the rest Irish Volunteers, captured the GPO (General Post Office) and other buildings in Dublin. They failed to capture Dublin Castle. Pádraig Pearse, a poet and schoolmaster, now commander-in-chief of the operation, read the *Proclamation of The Republic* outside the GPO. Passersby were furious – wasn't Ireland getting Home Rule after the war? "Stop breaking the windows!"

At first there was little military reaction to the Rising, mainly because the day was a holiday and there was a shortage of troops and armed police. Eventually the British Government sent in soldiers and heavy artillery. A gunboat fired from the Liffey and seriously damaged buildings along the quays including Liberty Hall. Many buildings were destroyed by fire as a result of the bombardment. After five days, with the GPO and surrounding buildings in flames, the republicans surrendered. Many people jeered at the prisoners as they were being led away.

Pearse surrenders near Parnell St.

Death toll: 142 British soldiers and police, 64 rebels, 254 civilians.

The GPO after the Rising

O'Connell Bridge after the Rising

POBLACHT NA H EIREANN.

THE PROVISIONAL GOVERNMENT
OF THE
IRISH REPUBLIC
TO THE PEOPLE OF IRELAND.

IRISHMEN AND IRISHWOMEN : In the name of God and of the dead generations fro m which she receives her old tradition of nationhood, Ireland, through us, summons her children to her flag and strikes for her. freedom.

Having organised and trained her manhood through her secret revolutionary organisation, the Irish Republican Brotherhood, and through her open military organisations, the Irish Volunteers and the Irish Citizen Army, having patiently perfected her discipline, having resolutely waited for the right moment to reveal itself, she now seizes that moment, and, supported by her exiled children in America and by gallant allies in Europe, but relying in the first on her own strength, she strikes in full confidence of victory.

We declare the right of the people of Ireland to the ownership of Ireland, and to the unfettered control of Irish destinies, to be sovereign and indefeasible. The long usurpation of that right by a foreign people and government has not extinguished the right, nor can it ever be extinguished except by the destruction of the Irish people. In every generation the Irish people have asserted their right to national freedom and sovereignty; six times during the past three hundred years they have asserted it in arms. Standing on that fundamental right and again asserting it in arms in the face of the world, we hereby proclaim the Irish Republic as a Sovereign Independent State, and we pledge our lives and the lives of our comrades-in-arms to the cause of its freedom of its welfare, and of its exaltation among the nations.

The Irish Republic is entitled to, and hereby claims, the allegiance of every Irishman and Irishwoman. The Republic guarantees religious and civil liberty, equal rights and equal opportunities to all its citizens, and declares its resolve to pursue the happiness and prosperity of the whole nation and of all its parts, cherishing all the children of the nation equally, and oblivious of the differences carefully fostered by an alien government, which have divided a minority from the majority in the past.

Until our arms have brought the opportune moment for the establishment of a permanent National Government, representative of the whole people of Ireland and elected by the suffrages of all her men and women, the Provisional Government, hereby constituted, will administer the civil and military affairs of the Republic in trust for the people.

We place the cause of the Irish Republic under the protection of the Most High God. Whose blessing we invoke upon our arms, and we pray that no one who serves that cause will dishonour it by cowardice, inhumanity, or rapine. In this supreme hour the Irish nation must, by its valour and discipline and by the readiness of its children to sacrifice themselves for the common good, prove itself worthy of the august destiny to which it is called.

Signed on Behalf of the Provisional Government,

THOMAS J. CLARKE.

SEAN Mac DIARMADA. THOMAS MacDONAGH.
P. H. PEARSE. EAMONN CEANNT.
JAMES CONNOLLY. JOSEPH PLUNKETT

Proclamation read by Patrick Pearse outside the GPO on Easter Monday 1916.
About 2,500 copies were printed in Liberty Hall the previous day. Some letters are not the correct size due to the difficulty in finding enough type at the time, without attracting unwanted attention.

Sinn Féin

Only days after the Rising 15 of the leaders were executed in Kilmainham Gaol. One of them, James Connolly, had to be tied to a chair as he had chest and ankle wounds and could not stand. These events made people more sympathetic towards the republicans.

In 1917 the government granted a general amnesty to those who took part in the Rising. There was a general election in 1918. The Sinn Féin party, founded in 1903 to seek independence, won a large majority of the Irish votes. This spelt the end of the Irish Parliamentary Party.

Sinn Féin refused to sit in Westminster and instead set up an Irish parliament – Dáil Éireann. From 1919 there were two governments ruling Ireland: the British and the Sinn Féin. Both held courts and collected taxes.

Sinn Féin is the only party that operates both in Northern Ireland and in the Republic. It has a large following in the former but is a minority party in the latter.

Eamon de Valera after the surrender.
De Valera was commander of a rebel unit in south Dublin. He was not executed after the Rising, perhaps because of his American birth (he was born in New York to an Irish mother and Spanish-Cuban father).

He became leader of Sinn Féin and then 'President of the Dáil'. He went to the US and argued for independence after World War 1, but his manner was inflexible and he achieved little in that regard. However, he travelled widely and was successful in fund-raising.

James Connolly was born in Edinburgh, Scotland, to Irish emigrant parents. Influenced by the poverty there (his father was a dung collector) he became a socialist. He edited socialist papers in Britain, then America. On coming to Ireland he joined with James Larkin in the Irish Transport and General Workers Union. Vladimir Lenin admired him, though the two never met.

Modern Irish socialists still regard Connolly as their 'spiritual' leader.

"Socialism is neither Protestant nor Catholic…; it is only human."

1. Fill in the blanks with the words below the text:

Sir Roger Casement

Roger Casement was born in Dublin and worked as a diplomat for the British government. He was knighted for his (a) _____ after he retired due to ill health. From the start of World War 1 he spent a lot of time in Germany (b) _____ to organize help for the Rising.

Captain Karl Spindler sailed the Aud, which was (c) _____ as a Norwegian trading ship, to Kerry, arriving on April 20, 1916. Casement (d) _____ in a u-boat. There was to be a pilot boat in Tralee Bay ready to guide the Aud and to offload the weapons, but it didn't (e) _____, as the date for the Rising had been changed. A British naval vessel stopped the Aud, and her captain searched her but found nothing – Spindler's friendly chatter and whiskey (f) _____ him. Meanwhile Casement got out of the u-boat and (g) _____ land in a rowboat. However, he was soon captured. The next day another British ship arrived and this time Spindler could not (h) _____ her captain. Before the Aud was brought into port Spindler got his men (i) _____, then exploded the ammunition and the ship sank.

Casement was tried in London. Evidence against him included his diary, in which he had written notes about his homosexual relationships. He was hanged in London (j) _____ August. Spindler spent some years in prison (k) _____ emigrating to the US.

that   off   before   trying   reached
distracted   services   disguised
appear   followed   fool

Roger Casement (hatless) with some of the crew on the German submarine U-19.

Casement was a British Consul in the Congo. There he inquired into the cruel treatment of the natives by representatives of the King of Belgium. His report caused the King to give up his personal ownership of the territory. He next worked in Brazil, where he reported on the exploitation of the Amazonian Indians. His report earned him a knighthood and forced the British rubber company to close their business.

Women of the Rising

1. Countess Markievicz

Constance Gore-Booth came from a rich unionist landlord family that had a large estate near Westport. Her home, Lissadell House, was often visited by W.B. Yeats. While studying art in Paris Constance met a Polish count whom she later married, hence her title. She became interested in the nationalist movement and abandoned her upper class lifestyle in order to help the poor. She started a boy scout organisation which included military training among its activities.

Markievicz joined Connolly's army because he, unlike other leaders of the Rising, allowed women to have equal status with men (remember that women did not have the right to vote until 1918). During the Rising Markievicz was second in command in St. Stephen's Green.

After her release from prison she campaigned in the election with the Sinn Féin party and she became the first woman MP (member of parliament). However, she did not sit in the parliament in Westminster but sat in the new Dáil Éireann in Dublin.

Having given all her possessions to the poor, she died penniless in a Dublin hospital in 1927. Being opposed to the Anglo-Irish Treaty (see page 88) she was not given a state funeral.

Lissadell House, Westport, now owned by Constance Cassidy and Eddie Walsh

2. Maud Gonne

Maud Gonne was the daughter of an Irish colonel in the English army. She studied in Paris, where she had a boyfriend, Lucien Millevoye (already married), a journalist. She had two daughters by him, the first one dying at the age of three. She brought up the second one as her niece. In 1898 she left Millevoye and started protesting against English rule in Ireland. W.B. Yeats fell in love with her and proposed marriage a

Gonne (centre) with members of her organization

number of times but she turned him down. Instead she married Major John McBride, who had fought for the Afrikaners in South Africa and who would later be a signatory of the Proclamation of Independence. She set up a women's group, Inghinidhe na hÉireann (Daughters of Ireland), to help the poor children of Dublin and to promote Irish independence. She was imprisoned in London (with Countess Markievicz) in 1918 and in Dublin by the new Irish government in 1923. She remained a member of Sinn Féin until her death in 1953.

One of Gonne's sons, Seán McBride, was a leading member of the IRA until he resigned in 1937. He was a founder of Amnesty International. He became Assistant Secretary-General of the United Nations, and won the Nobel Peace Prize in 1974.

3. Elizabeth O'Farrell

Elizabeth O'Farrell, a young nurse, was a member of Cumann na mBan (Women's League), an auxiliary organization for the Irish Volunteer Force. She was 17 when she was looking after the wounded James Connolly in the GPO. The day before the surrender, when the GPO was being heavily bombarded, Patrick Pearse ordered all the women to leave, but O'Farrell and others insisted on staying.

Elizabeth was the messenger who went to the British with a white flag, and later accompanied Pearse when he surrendered to General Lowe. She also delivered the surrender orders from Pearse and Connolly to the other rebel units around the city.

70 women were arrested and imprisoned after the Rising.

The wedding of Grace Gifford and Joseph Plunkett

Grace Gifford and Joseph Plunkett, one of the leaders of the Rising, became engaged to be married in December 1915, naming Easter Sunday as their wedding day. Of course, that day became impossible for their wedding. During the Rising Joseph fought in the GPO while Grace was a messenger for the rebels.

Before Plunkett was sentenced to death he told Grace that they would marry in prison. On 3 May Grace went to Grafton Street and bought a wedding ring. Joseph got permission to marry, and Grace was called to Kilmainham Gaol at 6 p.m. She was kept waiting until 11.30 p.m., then brought to the prison chapel where she and Joseph were married. The only other people in the chapel besides the priest were two soldiers, one holding a candle (the gaslights weren't working in the prison). After the wedding Joseph was handcuffed and taken back to his cell.

Grace was allowed see Joe again at 2 a.m. for ten minutes, but there were soldiers with them in his cell. At 3.30 a.m. the execution took place.

Grace had come from a unionist family in Dublin but became interested in the nationalist cause while still a young girl. After meeting Joseph she became a Catholic. Her parents did not approve of her republican sympathies and were unaware of her marriage.

Joseph Plunkett was a writer and friend of Patrick Pearse. He suffered from tuberculosis, and in the GPO gave instructions from his sickbed (as did James Connolly after he was injured). He organised the evacuation from the burning GPO – Pearse was unable to concentrate as a result of six days with little sleep.

Grace remained a member of Sinn Féin until her death in 1955.

An artist's impression of the wedding in Kilmainham Gaol. The gaol and chapel have been restored and are open to the public.

2. *Match the supposed quotations with their speakers. The first one has been done.*

1) "We can't do Home Rule now; there's a war on." **d**
2) "They're not new but they'll do."
3) "We're not joining with Germany, just using Germany."
4) "Some rebellion! They can't even organize a pilot boat!"
5) "I may be a woman but I can shoot as well as any man."
6) "For independence, and for socialism, let's go!"
7) "Okay Elizabeth, take these surrender orders to all units now."
8) "Ha, ha! Now go to jail where you belong, vandals!"
9) "The best thing to do is make an example of them."
10) "That's the best gold ring we have, Miss."
11) "I do, although I'll be a widow after doing it."
12) "At least I won't need to worry about my illness any more."
13) "This place is freezing, and the lights don't work. What a job!"
14) "If you won't help us politically, at least make a donation."
15) "These schoolchildren can't learn because they're so hungry."
16) "I know I've asked you before, but I love you so much…"

a) Countess Markievicz
b) Joseph Plunkett
c) Grace Gifford
d) the Prime Minister of Great Britain
e) Molly Childers
f) Pádraig Pearse
g) a soldier in Kilmainham Gaol
h) W. B. Yeats
i) Karl Spindler
j) James Connolly
k) People observing captured rebels
l) Eamon de Valera
m) a jewellery shop assistant
n) Roger Casement
o) General Maxwell, who ordered the executions
p) Maude Gonne

20. THE WAR OF INDEPENDENCE

Michael Collins

Michael Collins

In 1919 the War of Independence (also called the Anglo-Irish war) began. The army of Sinn Féin, the IRA. (Irish Republican Army) under the leadership of Michael Collins, fought the British forces and the Irish police using guerrilla tactics.

The British sent over the 'Black and Tans', part-time and unemployed soldiers who were given a free hand in suppressing the IRA. The result was that they acted in an unprofessional and cruel manner. They were called Black and Tans because their uniform was half black and half tan (brown). The British also sent over a group of spies, code-named 'the Cairo Gang'. Michael Collins used his own spies in Dublin Castle to find out their names and where they lived, then he had them executed in their houses. For the first time ever, Irish spies knew more than the British ones.

Black and Tans

The 'Cairo Gang'

Michael Collins became Britain's 'most wanted man' because he was organizing all the assassinations and attacks, and yet he could not be captured. He used to cycle around Dublin without being recognized!

The War of Independence was a terrible time for many people. Some big houses owned by rich unionists were destroyed by the IRA. Ordinary policemen were targeted by the IRA because they represented British rule in Ireland. Many police stations were attacked, and their guns taken by the IRA. In reprisal for these attacks the Black

Part of Cork city burnt by Black and Tans

and Tans would often enter a nearby town, shoot or torture some suspects and burn many of the houses. Collins' house in Cork was burnt down by the Black and Tans.

Bloody Sunday

The worst day of the war was perhaps on Sunday 21 November 1920, known as 'Bloody Sunday'. That morning Collins' men executed 14 English spies, many of them in their bedrooms. That afternoon a group of police and Black and Tans entered Croke Park stadium and killed two players and ten spectators. Two more spectators were killed in the panic to leave the stadium. Two suspects died later in Dublin Castle.

Anglo-Irish Treaty

Soon after such horrific events the English government offered to negotiate with Sinn Féin. Eamon de Valera, leader of Sinn Féin and President of the Dáil, sent Collins to London in 1921 to meet with Prime Minister Lloyd George and Winston Churchill and others. These were tense times – an aeroplane was on standby to rescue Collins in case he was arrested.

After two months' negotiation the Irish delegation still could not decide whether to accept a treaty being offered. In the end Lloyd George warned that if they did not sign the treaty, war would be the likely result. Then Collins and his colleagues signed. This treaty resulted in the division of Ireland into two parts: Northern Ireland, which would remain in the United Kingdom but would be given its own parliament; and the 'Free State', the rest of the country which would be given a great degree of independence, although members of its government would have to swear an oath to the King. When Collins signed the treaty he said, "I have signed my death certificate."

The 1921 negotiations in Downing Street.
Collins (3rd from right) is seated opposite Lloyd George. Winston Churchill is at the window. On Collins' right is Arthur Griffith, founder of Sinn Féin.

When the signatories returned home de Valera refused to accept the treaty. He said he would insist on independence for all Ireland, and that he would never swear an oath to the king of a foreign country. He walked out of the Dáil with about half of the members. The rest of the Dáil accepted the treaty, but those who opposed it with de Valera – the anti-treaty members of Sinn Féin and the IRA – began to use violence.

Tasks (ch 20)

1. *On the map on pages 64-65 mark the boundary of Northern Ireland (the six counties of Derry, Antrim, Down, Armagh, Tyrone and Fermanagh). Use the map on page 37 to help you.*

2. *Match the items below.*

   1. type of warfare   a) artillery
   2. insist on   b) brown
   3. supporter of strong political link with England c) guerrilla
   4. agreement   d) unionist
   5. tan   e) promise
   6. a person who signs a document   f) treaty
   7. oath   g) act of revenge
   8. reprisal   h) demand
   9. big guns   i) aim/goal
   10. target   j) signatory

3. Fill in the blanks.

Collins and de Valera

Eamon de Valera, one of the leaders of the Rising, was not executed but was (a) _____ in England. Collins helped him to (b) _____ by sending in a duplicate (c) _____ hidden in a cake (a very old trick!). Collins supported de Valera as leader of Sinn Féin. (d) _____ de Valera was raising funds in America, Collins expertly commanded the War of Independence in Ireland. When de Valera returned there was some coldness between (e) _____ ; it seems de Valera had become (f) _____ of Collins' rise to fame. De Valera (g) _____ Collins to the negotiations in London, although Collins wanted de Valera to (h) _____ as he now had the title 'President of the Irish Republic'. Some people believe de Valera knew that the outcome of the negotiations (i) _____ make the signatories unpopular, so he didn't go (j) _____.

The Mansion House, Dublin.
Venue for the first Dáil in 1919,
now the Lord Mayor's residence.

Leinster House, Dublin. Location of the present
Dáil. Built in 1746 for the Earl of Kildare. Elements
of its façade can be seen on the White House in
Washington, which was designed by Irish
American James Hoban.

Stormont, Belfast.
Purpose-built in 1932
for the Northern Irish
Parliament.

QUESTIONS FOR VOCABULARY REVIEW, CHAPTERS 16-20

If you are working alone just see how many questions below you can answer.

Otherwise, teacher/quizmaster please copy the table on page 22, putting in the letters below. Then follow the instructions.

The number after each question refers to the page on which the word first appears in these chapters. The word may occasionally have a different form.

S1 A platform for hanging people. 69
F1 Money for an organization. 90
M An organization with a political purpose. 67
S2 A break-up between two people or two groups. 72

A   A relationship between a married and an unmarried person. 73
P1 To make a book or newspaper and sell it. 76
T   To put up with. Don't complain about 'difficult' people. 78
S3 You are this towards someone when you share their sadness. 81

P2 To ask someone to marry you. 84
F2 When you are annoyed because you can't get what you need. 70
S4 Judge: "One year in prison is your S". 85
E   Not liking someone because you want what they have. 90

D   A copy of a thing, e.g. a key. 90
B   A song that tells a story. 67
U   To join people, political groups, together. 71
J   To laugh at other people and call them fools. 79

21. THE CIVIL WAR

The Anglo-Irish Treaty was signed in Downing Street on 6 December 1921. Most of the people in Ireland were relieved that the violence had stopped and that at least some form of independence was now to be enjoyed. However, many republicans were not happy with it, for the following reasons: 1) Northern Ireland was to remain British; 2) the 26 southern counties were to be called the 'Irish Free State', not the 'Irish Republic'; 3) The Free State was to be a part of the British Commonwealth; 4) members of its government were to swear allegiance to the King.

The split

Michael Collins persuaded many of his supporters that the Treaty was "freedom to win more freedom later". However, Eamon de Valera, the head of the Irish 'government', refused to accept it. After some emotional debates in the Dáil a vote was taken on 7 January 1922: 64 members voted in favour of the Treaty, 57 voted against it. De Valera resigned from the Dáil and Collins was appointed head of the government which would take over from the British authorities. De Valera warned that there would be bloodshed.

Soon after the Treaty was ratified, British troops began leaving their barracks, to be replaced by the new Free State army. Dublin Castle was also handed over to Collins. Meanwhile de Valera travelled the country trying to build up support for himself and (anti-treaty) Sinn Féin.

Besides the split in the Dáil there was a more serious split in the IRA. The anti-treaty section captured the Four Courts in Dublin. The pro-treaty section and others formed the Free State army. At first Collins made no effort to remove the IRA from the Four Courts, but the British prime minister demanded that action be taken, so he ordered the building to be fired on with field guns borrowed from the British. After two days of shelling, and with many documents destroyed, the garrison surrendered.

The Four Courts being shelled

Control of other buildings in Dublin took five more days to achieve.

Collins was appointed Commander-in-chief of the Free State Army and organized the war against his former colleagues in the IRA. He became very sad to see brother fighting against brother and families broken up. Other towns saw more fighting, but the most serious opposition to Collins was in Cork, the county of his birth.

Field gun in O'Connell Street

Ambush

Many of the roads into Cork city were blocked by the (anti-treaty) IRA, and railway lines were mined. Nevertheless, Collins went there to have meetings with neutral IRA leaders. At Béal na Bláth (The Mouth of the Flowers) on 22 August 1922 Collins' convoy was ambushed. Collins' assistant ordered the drivers to accelerate away but Collins told them to stop. The machine gun on the armoured car jammed. As usual Collins did not think of his safety, got out of his car and stood in the road firing at the enemy. He was killed by a bullet through his head.

Collins' convoy at Béal na Bláth
(TV drama. © RTE stills library)

The Civil War continued for eight more months, with atrocities that were equal to if not worse than those committed during the Anglo-Irish war. For example, in December a member of the Dáil was murdered; the next day four IRA prisoners were taken out of prison and shot. By the end of the war 73 more republican prisoners had been executed by the Free State government. Anti-treaty forces also committed atrocities against some Protestants, forcing them to leave their homes.

On 24 May 1923 de Valera called on the IRA to lay down their arms, but promised that he would continue to fight with them for 'Irish freedom' in a different way. Thus ended a war that would poison Irish political life for generations.

Tasks (ch 21)

1. Fill in the blanks with the words below the text.

The Big Fight during the fighting

> *"The history of the boxing ring has never*
> *known a contest with such an amazing setting."*
> Sporting Chronicle, London

A world championship boxing match (light heavyweight) was arranged
to be (a) _____ in Dublin on St. Patrick's Day 1922 between the
title-holder, a French Senegalese by the name of 'Battling' Siki, and the
(b) _____, the Irishman Mike McTigue.

Siki could not get a visa to fight in England but as the Irish Free State
was an independent country the (c) _____ decided to take
advantage of the situation.

Some IRA prisoners had been cruelly executed by the Free State
government and as a (d) _____ the IRA and de Valera warned
all theatres to close down. The government ordered the theatres to stay
open, and they did so, nervously, with soldiers (e) _____ guard
and nobody inside. However, the La Scala theatre in O'Connell Street,
the venue for the boxing match (now a Penneys store) became booked
(f) _____ and the crowds, plus 500 security troops, filled the whole
street.

When Siki was being driven to the theatre he heard the IRA shooting
nearby. He thought it was just fireworks (g) _____ his
arrival! During the match the IRA set off a bomb behind the theatre in
an attempt to cut the electric power, but they destroyed the wrong
(h) _____. Two musicians in the cinema next door were thrown
from their seats by the power of the explosion. The main fight
continued.

During the match there was a soldier with a rifle standing at each
corner of the (i) _____ looking out at the audience. The fight went
the full 20 rounds and McTigue was declared the winner. The crowds
cheered in the streets.

The Free State government had also won its (j) _____.

celebrating   held   contender   keeping
reprisal   out   fight   cables   ring   promoters

2. Fill in the blanks. Some initial letters are given.

Cruel irony of Civil War 1: Erskine Childers

Erskine Childers was (a) _____ in London of Protestant Anglo-Irish parents. He was (b) _____ up by his uncle in Wicklow. He wrote *The Riddle of the Sands,* the first modern spy novel. He (c) i_____ guns into Howth in his boat, *Asgard*, in 1914 (see photo on page 78). During WW1 he was in the British Navy and won an (d) _____ for bravery. In 1919 he joined Sinn Féin and was (e) m_____ publicity manager. He became friends with Collins and de Valera.

He was one of the (f) neg_____ of the Treaty in London with Collins, but he (g) opp_____ the inclusion of the oath to the King. On his (h) r_____ he joined the anti-treaty section and continued writing publicity for them. After the (i) k_____ of Michael Collins in August 1922 the new government made a law whereby any anti-treaty person with a gun would be (j) ex_____.

In November of the same year Childers was arrested and (k) a_____of having a gun. He was found guilty and executed by firing squad. Before his (l) e_____ he told his son, also called Erskine, to forgive the people who had signed his death warrant.

The gun in his (m) poss_____ had been given to him by Michael Collins.

Childers' son became President of Ireland in 1973.

Cruel irony of Civil War 2: Kevin O'Higgins

Kevin O'Higgins and Rory O'Connor were good friends and (n) b_____ members of the Irish Volunteers, later Sinn Féin. They were (o) im_____ during the War of Independence. In 1921 O'Higgins got married and Rory O'Connor was his best (p) _____ at his wedding.

O'Higgins was pro-treaty: "I advise the people to trust to evolution rather than (q) re_____." He became Minister for Justice in the provisional government. O'Connor sided with the anti-treaty IRA and took (r) _____ the Four Courts.

In 1923 O'Higgins ordered the execution of 77 IRA prisoners, (s) inc_____ Rory O'Connor. In the same year O'Higgins' father was shot dead, and in 1927 O'Higgins himself was assassinated. On his death-bed he (t) fo_____ his attackers.

The Irish delegates at the Treaty negotiation in London. On the left is Arthur Griffith, founder of Sinn Féin. Collins is seated in the centre and behind him to his right is Erskine Childers. The disagreement among the delegates is visible in their facial expressions.

A steam train is derailed after a rail has been removed from the track by the anti-treaty IRA. Many derailments and attacks took place during the civil war.

Collins' funeral was one of the largest ever seen in Dublin. For part of the funeral only one flower was allowed on his coffin – a white lily from his fiancée, Kitty Kiernan.

Siki prepares to swing a punch at McTigue

Kevin O'Higgins' wedding photo. Rory O'Connor is on the right and de Valera is on the left.

22. FREE STATE AND REPUBLIC

Stability

In August 1923 a general election was held. The Sinn Féin party won 44 seats, and the pro-treaty party, Cumann na nGaedhael (Society of the Gaels), won 63 seats. De Valera and Sinn Féin refused to sit in the Dáil as a protest against the oath of allegiance to the King. They also protested against the separation of Ireland but there was no real suggestion as to how to tackle that issue.

Cumann na nGaedhael governed well in establishing a new state. Among their achievements were the setting up of an unarmed police force and the maintenance of law and order in those difficult times. When de Valera seemed to threaten violence he was imprisoned for a year. The IRA was made an illegal organization and any member found with a gun would be executed. There was little discussion about Northern Ireland, perhaps because there was so much concentration on law and order. When the line of the border was finally agreed even a small part of Donegal was added to the six counties. In return the British cancelled some debts.

The IRA continued their campaign. They blew up or damaged statues of British leaders. They even attacked people wearing poppies on 'Poppy Day', and pulled down Union Jacks.

Fianna Fáil

In 1926 de Valera formed a new party named Fianna Fáil (Soldiers of Destiny). Fianna Fáil won the election in 1932 (and was the strongest party in Ireland from then until 2009). He created the 'Constitution of Ireland' in 1937. He abolished the parliamentary oath to the King and cancelled debts owed by farmers to the British Exchequer. The British retaliated with economic sanctions against Irish exports, which affected the economy greatly.

De Valera dealt wisely with the IRA, on the one hand giving jobs in the Free State army and police to many of them, and releasing many prisoners, but on the other hand declaring the IRA illegal and interning many of its members during WW2. He was equally wise with the Catholic church, on the one hand declaring it 'special' in his Constitution, but on the other hand refusing to declare Ireland a 'Catholic State', which displeased the Pope.

De Valera was also skilful in his negotiations with Britain, winning back control of all the ports in the Free State before World War 2 began.

De Valera kept Ireland neutral during World War 2, which made Winston Churchill very angry but increased de Valera's popularity at home because this demonstrated the country's sovereignty.

Fianna Fáil was replaced in government by the main opposition party, Fine Gael (formerly Cumann na nGaedhael), for three years from 1948. In 1949 the Free State was declared a republic, and membership of the British Commonwealth was terminated.

Economically the Free State/republic suffered from trade sanctions, economic depression after WW2 and conservative social and economic policies. De Valera seemed to concentrate more on Irish culture than on the economy. He made Irish the official state language (with English); consequently, all civil servants had to pass an exam in Irish (De Valera had to brush up on it himself). Irish was also made a compulsory subject in schools. While Northern Ireland had a strong industrial base the south had to rely on agricultural exports and trade tariffs. The result was almost a constant outflow of emigrants, and luckily for those going to England they were granted the same social benefits as British citizens. Until the 1960's many poor city families lived in one-room flats and some children went barefoot.

Trade tariffs were dropped in the late 60's, and in 1973 Ireland joined the EU with Britain and Denmark.

The IRA

As the Free State stabilized, the IRA lost popular support and its numbers fell sharply. Still there was a lasting hatred of de Valera for having betrayed them, and they continued to carry out bombing raids in England and Ireland. Gradually its leaders looked to more socialist aims, in the manner of James Connolly, but not all its members seemed interested in this. Not until the 'Troubles' flared up in Northern Ireland did the IRA regain some of its motivation and popularity/notoriety.

After an IRA bomb explosion in Coventry, England, in 1939. Five people were killed.

Fill in the blanks. Some initial letters are given.

De Valera's constitution

In de Valera's constitution the Free State was renamed 'Ireland'. This was (a) <u>wel</u>_____ by most of its citizens, but people distinguish between 'the island of Ireland' and 'the Republic of Ireland' or 'the 26 counties'. The name *Éire* is often seen on mail from Britain.

Article 2 stated: 'The national (b) <u>ter</u>_____ consists of the whole island of Ireland.' This was only an aspiration, perhaps to keep popularity with republicans; Article 3 stated more (c) <u>pra</u>_____ that the laws of the state only applied to the 26 counties. However, the claim to the whole of Ireland did nothing to endear northern unionists, and in 1999 it was (d) <u>dro</u>_____ by referendum and replaced with expressions of harmony and friendship.

De Valera seemed to do little to court northern unionists. The Catholic church's 'special position' was noted in the constitution, and this would be another (e) <u>r</u>_____ for northern unionists to stay with Britain.

To be fair to de Valera, it could be said that he was simply acknowledging the respect (and power) that the Catholic church (f) _____ had, and being grateful that most hospitals and schools were run by religious orders at low cost to the state. It is not surprising then that censorship was (g) <u>str</u>_____ (many books, including Joyce's *Ulysses*, were banned), divorce was banned and the open sale of condoms was illegal until 1993 (the reduction of VAT on condoms was (h) <u>con</u>_____ by Catholic leaders in 2008).

The Blueshirts

General O'Duffy, former police commissioner, became leader of the 'National Guard', nicknamed 'Blueshirts'. They provided security for Cumann na nGaedhael meetings.

O'Duffy thought the Catholic church would support him, as it had supported fascists against communists elsewhere, but he got no backing from the church. De Valera banned his parades in 1933, and the organisation gradually died away.

O'Duffy raised an 'Irish Brigade' to fight for Franco but it achieved little. Other Irishmen fought against Franco, 80 of whom were killed.

Ireland's attitude to Word War One (WW1) veterans

During WW1 200,000 Irishmen served in the (British) army. They were encouraged to do so by John Redmond, the leader of the Irish Parliamentary party (in Westminster), because he believed this would ensure Home Rule and encourage unionists and nationalists to live in harmony. His brother Willie, aged 56, died in action in France. John became dispirited, especially at the rise of Sinn Féin. "The life of... an Irish politician is a long series of postponements, compromises, disappointments and disillusions...". He died in 1918. Some believe his parliamentary approach would have won results sooner and more peacefully than the violent approach used by the IRA.

Many Irish soldiers won bravery awards in WW1. However, on their return to nationalist Ireland they found that they were regarded as having fought for the enemy of Ireland. Some joined the IRA and the new Irish Free State army. Many found it hard to get a job. This negative attitude towards such men lasted for a long time, ending only in 1998 when Queen Elizabeth and President Mary McAleese unveiled the Irish Tower (see p18) at the Messines battle site in Belgium. Relationships were further restored with the visit of the Queen to Ireland in 2011 – the first visit by a British monarch in 100 years.

Queen Elizabeth praises President McAleese for her work in restoring relationships

Tom Crean

Tom Crean was one of those Irishmen who served in the Royal forces but got little recognition back home for his bravery. Some years after joining the Royal Navy he was recruited by Robert Scott in 1911 and later Ernest Shackleton for their Antarctic expeditions. Once, he walked 56km alone in the snow and ice to get help for his team. For this and other feats he was awarded polar medals by King George V in Buckingham Palace.

Tom with pups born on the *Endurance*. Photo by Frank Hurley, the ship's photographer.

On his return home to Cork he opened up a pub, 'The South Pole Inn', but never spoke about his time in the Navy; he knew that some people just didn't want to know. His brother, a policeman, was killed in an IRA ambush in 1920. Tom died of a burst appendix in 1938.

23. NORTHERN IRELAND

Unionism

At the turn of the 20th century most Protestants in the north of Ireland were in favour of continuing the connection with Britain. Every time Home Rule was debated in London the northern unionists reacted strongly against it. The Conservative Party supported them. Winston Churchill's father said, "Ulster will fight, Ulster will be right."

Carson, centre, attends a 'No Home Rule' rally in Derry in 1912

Edward Carson, a Protestant lawyer from Dublin but now working in London decided to support the unionists. In 1912 he and James Craig arranged that people in Belfast could sign a document declaring their willingness to fight against Home Rule (they said Home Rule would mean 'Rome Rule'). Almost a million people signed.

Carson and James Craig then formed the Ulster Volunteers – a resistance force of 100,000 men – and imported 35,000 rifles from Germany without any interference from the police. The government in Westminster was embarrassed and feared civil war. After WW1 six northern counties were given their own parliament, opened in 1921 by King George V. Divisions remained deep – most Catholics were republicans/nationalists and most Protestants were unionists – and violence continued. In 1922 alone 232 people were killed in riots.

King George V arrives to open the Northern Ireland Parliament

The unionists were determined to hold on to power. The voting system was arranged so that unionists would always be in the majority. The religious breakdown was 820,000 Protestants and 430,000 Catholics, yet unionists won 40 of the 52 seats. Craig declared in 1934, "We are a Protestant Parliament and a Protestant State." Many institutions of the new state (e.g. housing, education, police) were biased in favour of unionists, and with unemployment rising to 25% the Protestant-owned companies such as Harland and

Wolff Shipyard (where the Titanic was built) employed mainly Protestants.

Workers view propellers of the Titanic in the Harland and Wolff Shipyard in Belfast

Leonardo DiCaprio and Kate Winslet in the film 'Titanic' (1997)

More riots and more deaths occurred, but during World War 2 the unemployment situation improved. Harland and Wolff produced over 200 ships, the linen mills became world famous, and of course because the Free State was neutral the Northern Ireland ports became very busy, especially when used as stop-overs for American troops. After the war more Catholics benefited by being employed by new international companies, and all shared in the benefits of the new social welfare system introduced by the British government.

Women working in a Belfast linen mill, 1940

When Terence O'Neill became Prime Minister of Northern Ireland in 1963 he said he would "build bridges between the two traditions." However, not many unionists approved. The flying of a tricolour in west Belfast caused a riot (it was illegal to fly the flag of the Republic in Northern Ireland). Ian Paisley formed the DUP (Democratic Unionist Party), opposed to any contact with Dublin and any form of ecumenism. He became leader of his own Presbyterian church.

Local government was still biased against Catholics, whose main complaint was discrimination in housing and employment. The Civil Rights Association was founded in 1967 and organised protest marches similar to those in the US. In 1969 the police brutally baton-charged the march in Derry. This was seen world-wide on television.

The Troubles

The period of conflict known as the 'Troubles' began in August 1969. The residents of the Bogside area of Derry protested against the Apprentice Boys' march on the walls of the city. The police attempted to disperse the protestors but these began rioting against them. The riots lasted for days and spread to Belfast. The police in Derry became exhausted and the British army was called in to restore order. By the time order was restored 8 people had been killed and 750 injured. In addition, 1,505 Catholic families and 315 Protestant ones had been driven from their homes, either through burning or intimidation.

The Provisional IRA

The Northern Ireland government blamed the IRA for the violence, but in fact many nationalists blamed the IRA for doing nothing, especially for not protecting them. The Official IRA at this time was not militant, so a large breakaway group, the Provisional IRA, was formed. At first the 'Provos' as they were called, just defended the Catholic areas, but later they

IRA 'checkpoint'. Several 'no-go' areas existed in republican and loyalist districts.

started their 'war' to remove British control from Northern Ireland. They killed soldiers, policemen, loyalist paramilitaries, and 'informers'. They also carried out numerous bombings and punishment beatings.

Internment

In 1971 internment (imprisonment without trial) began. In the early hours of August 9th British soldiers swept into nationalist areas and arrested 342 men. Many of those arrested had no connections with the IRA, and within 48 hours 116 of those arrested were released.

In the same 48 hour period there was a violent reaction in the streets and 17 people were killed, of whom 10 were Catholic civilians shot dead by the British Army. In the following weeks about 7,000 people, the majority of them Catholics, were forced to leave their homes. Many of them moved to the Republic. Internment was to continue until December 1975. During that time 1,981 people, mostly Catholic, were interned.

Bloody Sunday

Bloody Sunday in Derry was on 30 January 1972. British soldiers opened fire during a banned civil rights march, killing fourteen people. At the funerals many politicians from north and south joined thousands of mourners. In Dublin the British Embassy was burned to a shell, without much interference from the Garda. Two months later the British government

Civil Rights demonstrators throw stones at British soldiers in Derry/Londonderry, 1972

closed the Northern Ireland parliament. (In 2010 British Prime Minister David Cameron apologised for the 'unjustifiable' killings.)

The IRA carried out a total of 1,300 bombings in 1972, and 479 people died in the Troubles in that year, more than in any other year of the conflict. 4,000 extra British troops were brought into Northern Ireland to dismantle the barricades that had been built in 'no go' areas.

Hunger strikes

Imprisoned IRA members demanded to be treated as soldiers and to be allowed to wear their own clothes, but Margaret Thatcher, the 'iron lady' Prime Minister, said they would be treated as criminals.

In 1981 a hunger strike was begun by Bobby Sands, a popular IRA member in prison. There was a general election in April and Bobby Sands' name was put forward as a candidate. He was elected to parliament and became Bobby Sands, MP. Of course, he could not go to Westminster but the publicity generated by his election brought worldwide attention to the North and helped the Sinn Féin party. After that a law was made which disallowed a prisoner from standing for election to parliament.

Bobby Sands was the first of ten republican prisoners to die during the hunger strike, which lasted from March to October 1981.

In France five towns have streets named after Bobby Sands.

The funeral of Bobby Sands. Gerry Adams, Sinn Féin leader, is among the coffin bearers.

A previous IRA hunger striker was **Terence MacSwiney**, the Lord Mayor of Cork. His hunger strike, to the death, lasted for 74 days while he was in Brixton Prison in England in 1920. He gained a lot of attention worldwide, with protests in Europe and America. Indian leaders like Mahatma Gandhi counted him among their influences.

Atrocities

Between 1969 and 1998 almost 3,600 people died in the Troubles. While most of the violence took place in Northern Ireland, some serious bombings also occurred in England, including the bombing of a hotel where Margaret Thatcher was staying. There were also two major car bombings in the Republic, supposedly the work of the UVF, which claimed 33 lives and injured 300.

Some other atrocities during the Troubles were:

- The murder by the UVF of three members of a music band on their way home south across the border in 1975.
- In 1987, the killing by the IRA of 11 civilians at a memorial service in Enniskillen for soldiers who died in WW1 and WW2.
- In 1998, the killing of 29 people, including two Spanish tourists, by a car bomb in Omagh, planted by the RIRA (Real IRA, against the Good Friday Agreement). "Northern Ireland's worst atrocity" – BBC.
- For three months in 2001, the stone-throwing at parents and police protecting children as they walked to a Catholic girls' school in a Protestant area. A small bomb was also thrown, injuring policemen.

The peace process

In 1985 there was a significant political development: the signing of the Anglo-Irish Agreement by Margaret Thatcher, UK Prime Minister, and Garret FitzGerald, Taoiseach (Prime Minister) of the Republic. The unionists opposed it, seeing it as a step towards joint sovereignty. Sinn Féin also opposed it because it gave validity to Northern Ireland. Violence followed but the Agreement survived for some years.

SDLP leader John Hume had meetings with Sinn Féin leader Gerry Adams. In 1994 a ceasefire was declared by the IRA

Ian Paisley, leader of the DUP, the largest unionist party, refused to enter into talks with 'Sinn Féin/IRA' until 2005

and later by the militant loyalists. The unionists demanded that the IRA decommission (destroy) their weapons immediately, but they refused. Eventually, with persuasion from US President Bill Clinton, most unionists agreed to attend talks.

When Tony Blair's Labour Party got into government he was eager to solve the conflict. In October 1997 formal peace talks began, chaired by US Senator George Mitchell.

The Good Friday Agreement

On Good Friday (the Friday before Easter) in 1998 the main political parties signed an agreement to form an **Assembly** to govern Northern Ireland. This would be composed of nationalist and unionist parties. Included in the agreement was an amnesty for imprisoned terrorists who would give up violence. In the Republic, the people voted to drop the constitutional claim to the 'whole of Ireland'.

John Hume, leader of the SDLP, and David Trimble, leader of the Ulster Unionist Party, were jointly awarded the Nobel Peace Prize.

Mistrust continued, however, and only in 2005 when independent inspectors confirmed that the IRA had decommissioned their weapons did Ian Paisley agree to join the Assembly. In 2006 when Sinn Féin agreed to support the PSNI (Police Service of Northern Ireland – formerly called the Royal Ulster Constabulary) Paisley's DUP entered into shared government with them and other parties.

The Northern Ireland Assembly continues, although its work is hindered by disagreements between unionists and nationalists. However, progress is being made, however slowly, and tourism has grown well.

One tourist attraction is the 'Peace Walls' which were built to prevent clashes between Catholic and Protestant neighbourhoods, even after the Good Friday agreement. A small number have been dismantled, but many residents still express anxiety about the dismantling of any more.

Lyra McKee, a popular journalist, shot dead in a 'New IRA' riot in Derry in 2019

Tourists at a 'Peace Wall' in Belfast. Some peace walls have been dismantled, but up to 40 still remain. Many have colourful artwork.

Tasks (ch 23)

1. Complete the crossword.

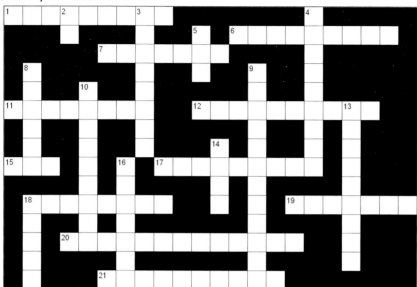

ACROSS
1 A movement promoting unity between Christian churches. (9)
6 To take apart (equipment, furniture etc.). (9)
7 A ceremony for a dead person. (7)
11 The northern unionists were prepared to fight against this. (4,4)
12 The Free State operated by this policy during World War 2. (10)
15 This nation's army used Northern Ireland as a stopover during WW2. (3)
17 People not in military service. (9)
18 A cruel and violent act, usually done in wartime. (8)
19 A pardon for a prisoner. (7)
20 Most unionists are members of this religion. (13)
21 Imprisonment without trial. (10)

DOWN
2 A person elected to Westminster. (2)
3 This republican party opposed the Anglo-Irish Agreement. (4,4)
4 More of these people got jobs after World War 2 due to the growth of international business in Northern Ireland. (9)
5 Bobby Sands died because he refused to do this. (3)
8 A nickname for the breakaway, more violent group of the IRA. (6)
9 The act of bullying someone using threats. (12)
10 The design of the Irish flag. (9)
13 The Irish word for 'prime minister'. (9)
14 Unfair judgment based on personal reasons. (4)
16 This American persuaded unionists to enter peace talks. (7)
18 The first part of a word meaning 'partly English'. (5)

2. Match the descriptions of the organizations below with the circles on the next page. One (number 6) has been done.

1. Formed in 1914, this political party was, and many say still is, in close contact with the IRA.

2. Existed from 1970 to 1992 as a part-time and full-time defence regiment of the British army, but consisting of local people. 192 of its members were killed by the Provisional IRA.

3. Formed in 1966 to fight against the IRA, it later included Catholic civilians as targets. They killed 15 Catholics in a bar in Belfast in 1971. A breakaway group, the LVF (Loyalist Volunteer Force), engaged in feuds with it in the 90's. It declared an end to its military activities in 2007.

4. Two prominent members of this paramilitary organisation were Gerry Adams (people believe) and Martin McGuinness. The latter became Deputy First Minister of the Northern Ireland Assembly.

5. A paramilitary defence association formed in 1971 to resist unification with the Republic. It was banned in 1992. Notorious for killing 8 customers in a Catholic bar on Halloween in 1993, shouting 'trick or treat'. They said it was in retaliation for an IRA bomb which killed 9 people in a Protestant street the week before.

6. A political party formed for non-violent nationalists. One of its leaders, John Hume, won the Nobel Peace Prize with David Trimble, leader of the UUP. It has the word 'social' but not 'republican' in its title.

7. A unionist party willing to accept compromise, but it consequently risked being isolated by the 'No' unionists. Its leader shared the Nobel Peace Prize with John Hume in 1998.

8. A 'national' Republican military organisation which broke away from the IRA in 1974. Three of its members died in the hunger strike. It was responsible for over 100 deaths, some involving smuggling rackets. It declared a ceasefire in 1998 but it was not until 2009 that it declared an end to violence. 'Liberation' was one of its aims.

9. This organisation split from the IRA in 1997 as they did not agree with the ceasefire. They continue their aim to achieve an all-Ireland republic by violent means. Their name implies that the IRA had become 'unreal'. A later group implies that the IRA had become too 'old'.

10. The 'Ulster Says No' party founded by Ian Paisley and now with a strong representation in the Northern Ireland Assembly.

11. The former name for the police force of Northern Ireland, which is now the PSNI. Among other changes was the removal of the word 'Royal'.

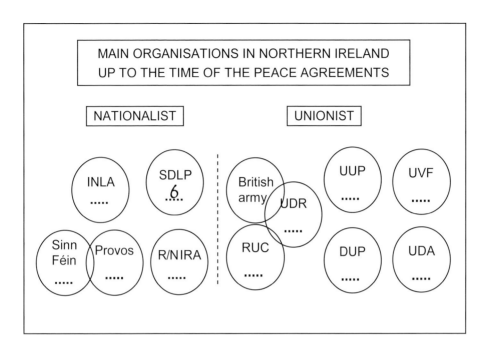

MAIN ORGANISATIONS IN NORTHERN IRELAND
UP TO THE TIME OF THE PEACE AGREEMENTS

NATIONALIST

UNIONIST

INLA
.....

SDLP
.6.

British
army

UDR
.....

UUP
.....

UVF
.....

Sinn
Féin
.....

Provos
.....

R/N IRA
.....

RUC
.....

DUP
.....

UDA
.....

The title *Óglaigh na hÉireann* (Irish Volunteers) was used by the Irish Volunteers from 1914. It was adopted by the IRA in 1919. Since 1922 the name and badge have been officially used by the Irish Defence Forces. The title is still also used by dissident republican groups.

Another ambiguity is in the letters FF. They stand for *Fianna Fáil* (Soldiers of Destiny/Ireland). This is also the name of a large political party.

UVF Banner.
The original Ulster Volunteers were founded in 1912 to resist Home Rule. Many thousands of their members were killed at the Battle of the Somme in WW1.

The name was adopted in 1966 by an anti-IRA/Catholic organisation.

24. CHANGES

From boom 1 ...

Pre-1990 Ireland was a relatively poor country, but by 2004 Ireland's GDP* per capita had risen to become Europe's second highest. This economic boom became known as the 'Celtic Tiger'. Below are listed some factors which caused it.

1. For many years the Republic of Ireland received aid from the EU. In 2003 it got the highest amount (per head) of any European country.
2. Ireland's young, English speaking population made it attractive to multinational corporations like Intel, Apple, Dell, Microsoft, Google, Pfizer and others. Another attraction was Ireland's low corporate tax rate of 12.5 percent.
3. The demand for housing rose, due to tax incentives for property investors, the ease of getting a mortgage, and the increasing number of immigrants. House prices quadrupled from 1997 to 2007. Many builders became millionaires, and just kept building.

Carrick-a-rede rope bridge in Co. Antrim. Tourism in Northern Ireland has grown dramatically since the signing of the Good Friday agreement.

... to bust

From 2008 Ireland's economy, and much of the world's, went into recession (recession = negative GDP growth over 6 months).

High salaries were also affecting Ireland's competitiveness – public sector salaries are above the EU average; the Prime Minister of Ireland earns more than the President of the US – some companies started relocating to Asian or East European countries where labour is cheaper, e.g. Dell moved its manufacturing plant from Limerick to Poland. With other factory closures unemployment soon rose from 4% to 15%. 5,500 jobs were lost every week in 2009.

House prices dropped, leaving many investors in debt. Many building companies also went bankrupt. Too many houses had been built. By 2010 over 320,000 new homes were unoccupied.

As in the US and elsewhere, banks had given mortgages too easily,

*GDP = Gross Domestic Product, a way of measuring a country's economy. It is basically the value of all goods and services produced in the country in one year.

and many of the borrowers could not pay back the loans. The Irish bank regulations and controls turned out to be very weak. In fact, there were some scandals; for example, one bank lent money to investors to buy shares – in the same bank! It also took a deposit of €7bn from another large bank to make it look strong – for one day!

As with Greece, Spain and Portugal, Ireland had to accept a 'bailout' (loan) from the 'Troika' – the European Commission (EC), the European Central Bank (ECB) and the International Monetary Fund (IMF). For Ireland, this was in 2010, for €67.5bn, used mainly to save the banks. The main condition was that government spending had to be reduced drastically. Consequently, taxes were increased and cuts were made in social welfare benefits and public services, e.g. the police, health, education, etc. Many homeowners could not afford to pay their mortgages and faced eviction.

Br. Kevin Crowley at his Friary in Dublin, where 700 meals are distributed each day and 1,500 food parcels each week

... to boom 2?

After three years Ireland had fulfilled the conditions of the Troika and needed less supervision. Confidence soon returned to the financial markets and by 2018 Ireland's GDP was the highest in Europe (4% annual growth). More multinationals set up or expanded in Ireland, e.g. Facebook, Google, Pfizer. Indigenous companies also grew, causing the unemployment rate to return to a low of 4.8%.

However, the fresh demand for houses was not met, and consequently prices rose rapidly, again almost mirroring the 'Celtic Tiger' days. People on low incomes were unable to purchase a house or pay the rising rents. From 2012 to 2019 homelessness (adults and children in emergency accommodation) increased from 3,300 to 10,000.

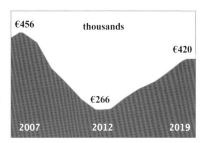

€456   thousands

€420

€266

2007   2012   2019

Average house prices in Dublin, 2007-2019

Besides homelessness, another contradiction to Ireland's economic recovery is its growing national debt, the highest in the EU in 2019, when every man, woman and child in the Republic owed €42,800.

Brexit

The UK's decision to leave the EU will have long lasting effects for Ireland. The majority of people in Northern Ireland voted to remain in the EU. The border between Northern Ireland and the Republic (with 275 crossings) is likely to cause trade and political headaches. Some say a **united Ireland** would be a solution to this problem; however, that is a sensitive issue as many unionists are against it. In Northern Ireland young teenage Catholics (45%) now outnumber Protestant ones (34%). Eligible Britons (those with an Irish grandparent or living in Northern Ireland) got 200,000 Irish passports in 2018.

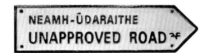

Not all 275 crossings were 'approved' by customs officers before Ireland and Britain joined the EU in 1973. During the 'Troubles' in Northern Ireland over 100 of these roads were blocked by the British army to restrict IRA movement.

Demographics

Since Ireland became attractive to immigrants from the new EU countries and beyond, along with its normal growth and returning emigrants its population (north and south) has increased from five million to six-and-a-half million in the past 20 years.

Alcohol

Guinness, Baileys and various whiskeys provide good export earnings for Ireland. Also, a lot of alcohol is consumed domestically. However, alcohol is blamed for many social problems:

> Nearly half of all murders committed in Ireland are alcohol related. One in three road deaths is alcohol related. 25% of domestic violence is drink-fuelled. 25% of people admitted to A & E departments have consumed large amounts of alcohol. Liver disease has increased by 148% over the past decade.

More alcohol is being consumed in people's homes now. Two pubs have closed every week since 2012. Causes cited are the high prices of beer in pubs, severe drink-driving penalties and the smoking ban (in 2004 Ireland was the first country in the world to introduce the ban in all work places).

Many young people tend to associate drunkenness with happiness, even with 'Irishness'. Drinking shots (small strong drinks that you 'down in one') and binge drinking (drinking fast to get drunk) have caused many problems. Ireland comes second, behind Austria, in binge drinking statistics (WHO 2014).

Drugs

As cocaine and guns have become cheaper, crime gangs have grown in number and viciousness. Drug-related criminality is constantly growing, and this situation is not helped by the reduction in Garda overtime, in effect since the recession. The Garda is an unarmed police force. Ireland's cocaine usage is third after the US and Spain (EMCDDA 2019).

On the bright side...

Ireland's film industry remains healthy, with studios in Wicklow and Belfast.

Ireland's food products are highly regarded; Ireland is the largest exporter in Europe of infant formula (milk powder).

Many software entrepreneurs have set up their own successful businesses.

Famous names: Saoirse Ronan and Rory McIlroy

The Irish are 'the happiest people in Europe' according to regular surveys. They also spend the most on Valentine's Day.

Religion

There has been a fall-off in church attendances for the main Christian religions, although there is still a preference for church baptisms, weddings and funerals. About 85% of elementary schools are of Catholic patronage. Islam is the fastest growing religion in Ireland. The number of atheists and agnostics also continues to grow.

Irish missionaries and charity workers contribute greatly to developing nations. Examples include Fr. Shay Cullen, who has helped children and human trafficking victims in the Philippines, Niall Mellon, whose trust has built 25,000 houses and 16 schools in South Africa, and Sr. Orla Treacy, who is helping families and combating forced marriages of young girls in South Sudan.

Orla Treacy, a Loreto nun from Bray, receives the International Women of Courage Award from US First Lady Melania Trump

Two referenda reflect the weakening of Catholic influence on Irish life: 1) in 2015 Ireland introduced same-sex marriage; 2) in 2018 abortion became no longer illegal. This is in contrast to Northern Ireland, where at time of publication attitudes remain more conservative, especially among unionists.

QUESTIONS FOR VOCABULARY REVIEW, CHAPTERS 21-24

If you are working alone just see how many questions below you can answer.

Otherwise, teacher/quizmaster please copy the table on page 24, putting in the letters below. Then follow the instructions.

The number after each question refers to the page on which the word first appears in these chapters.

Sometimes two words are required, hence the two letters together.

I1 Baby. 113
M Money you borrow from a bank to buy a house. 110
A1 A person who doesn't believe in God. 113
B Prohibit. 99

I2 Away from / outside of the main activity. 108
A2 Bad things done by people against people. 93
BD Drinking fast to get drunk. 112
S To promise in a formal way. 92

C1 A number of activities to achieve an aim. 97
BM At a wedding, the groom's (man to be married's) assistant. 95
U Not carrying weapons. 97
C2 As a result. 98

A3 An expressed hope, a wish. 99
V A place for a meeting or a performance. 94
C3 Both sides accepting less than originally demanded. 108
C4 An adjective meaning 'business'. 110

KEY TO TASKS

1. THE STONE AGE
1. BONES and ASHES

2. a) structure   b) cliff   c) well   d) forts   e) mined   f) tin   g) imported   h) can

2. THE CELTS
1. 1g   2f   3b   4c   5i   6e   7j   8a   9d   10h

2. a) speak   b) France   c) connection   d) spoken   e) seen   f) name
g) based   h) oral   i) tribes   j) evidence   k) slaves

3. THE GOLDEN AGE: CHRISTIANITY
1. 1c   2h   3f   4a   5e   6j   7i   8g   9d   10b

2. To the teacher: before announcing 'True' or 'False' it's fun to read the reasoning aloud to the learners, so that the logic reveals itself slowly.

1. False. During the ice age it was too cold to get to Ireland, and when the ice melted there was no land bridge between Britain and Ireland. There are no snakes in Ireland because they can't swim!

2. Doubtful. The clover is larger than the shamrock, so why didn't Patrick use that? The first mention of the shamrock as a symbol of Ireland is in the 18th century. Most information about Patrick is taken from his letter 'Confessions'; there is no reference to any trefoil in it.

   The large clover with a white flower is *Trifolium repens*. The small clover, the shamrock, with a yellow flower, is *Trifolium minus*. The Irish *seamair óg* means 'clover small/young'.

   A four-leaved clover (or four-leaf clover) is said to bring good luck. The shamrock is a symbol of Ireland and not a lucky charm, although souvenir makers are happy to forget this.

3. True. Patrick spent the last years of his life in the north of Ireland, and some writings (which also say he was 122 years old!) mention Downpatrick as his resting place. There are no remains, but the important word for the answer is 'believed'.

4. False. He couldn't have worn a mitre (bishop's hat) because bishops only started wearing these in the 11th century.

5. False. Ireland was a poor country for a long time. Poor people don't have time for parades. The first St. Patrick's Day observance was held in Boston in 1737. The first parade was in New York in 1762. The first parade in Ireland was in Waterford in 1903.

6. False. Belfast City Council only started to support a parade in 2006. St. Patrick's Day wasn't a holiday in Northern Ireland until 2000.

7. False. Pubs in Ireland were not allowed to open on St. Patrick's Day until 1970.

8. False. The Chicago river is slow moving, which makes it ideal for dyeing, which has been done since 1962. The tidal movements in the Liffey make it impracticable (so far).

9. False. Irish people at home don't like being 'too Irishy'. Only in Irish pubs abroad – there are over 6,000 of them – does this happen to any extent.

10. True.*

11. True. This was started in 2019.*

12. True. This was started by Michelle Obama.*

*These customs may have changed since time of publication. If in doubt please check.

3. a) old   b) where   c) one   d) both/these/ both these   e) in   f) for
g) allowed   h) same

4. THE VIKINGS
a) hands   b) those   c) Its   d) look   e) more   f) out   g) potato
h) Another   i) 19.2   j) 1980

5. THE NORMANS
1. Christ Church Cathedral

2. a) stone   b) wooden   c) consisted   d) surrounding   e) examples
f) centuries   g) enjoyed   h) respected   i) stingy   j) area

VOCABULARY REVIEW, CHAPTERS 1-5
brooch   manufacture   hunt   Lent
fort   tin   dye   armour
swamp   raid   obey   victory
stingy   peat   helmet   pagan

6. HENRY VIII
1. a) had   b) to   c) at   d) would   e) Besides   f) from   g) so   h) have
i) had   j) with   k) against

2. a) whenever (= every time)   b) once (or when) (*Once* means 'after waiting' or 'when something is completed'. *When* does not show this extra meaning).
c) when (= at that time)

7. THE SPANISH ARMADA
a) military   b) cooperate   c) high   d) which   e) extra   f) even   g) just   h) less

8. ELIZABETH INCREASES HER CONTROL OF IRELAND
1. a) century   b) brought   c) familiar   d) decided   e) costing   f) due
g) entrance   h) allow   i) threat   j) hand   k) buried   l) divorced
m) distributed

2. a) If King Philip <u>had</u> known more about the English ships, he <u>would/might have</u> built faster ships.

b) If the Earls <u>had</u> remained in Ulster, the plantation <u>would/might have</u> been much smaller.

c) If Henry <u>had not</u> insisted on getting a divorce, the Church of England <u>would/might not</u> now be in existence.

d) If King Philip had helped O'Neill, Ireland <u>would/might</u> now <u>be</u> a part of Spain.

e) (Suggested answer) If the plantation had been smaller, <u>Northern Ireland would not have had so much trouble</u>.

<small>(Note: the comma after the 'if' clause is not normally used in English, but is included here for clarity.)</small>

9. PLANTATION

Why was Sir Walter Raleigh the first man to smoke tobacco and plant potatoes in Ireland? Because he had brought these plants from America to Europe. In fact, Ireland was the first European country in which the potato was planted.

a) entirely   b) Connaught   c) returned   d) allowed   e) most   f) changed
g) gratitude

10. THE PIRATE QUEEN

1. a) returning   b) pay   c) disturbed   d) against   e) kidnapped
f) apologised   g) promise   h) unexpected   i) followed

2. (Note: *may have* or *could have* are alternatives to *might have*.)
1. might have   2. should have   3. should *not* have   4. can't have
5. must have   6. must have   7. might have (*must have* is also possible)

VOCABULARY REVIEW, CHAPTERS 6-10
surrender   palace   exile   channel
naked   ammunition   negotiate   unfaithful
cloak   survivor   hearse   ignore
enforce   timber   hide   thorn

11. KINGS IN CONFLICT

1. a) place   b) leader   c) ammunition   d) defence   e) supplies   f) captured
g) surrender   h) signed   i) allowed   j) known

2. Firstly: James II and Mary Stuart were children of Charles I. So,
a) William III's father, William II, was James II's brother-in-law.
b) William III was James's son-in-law, also his nephew.

3. 1d   2f   3a   4h   5g   6j   7e   8c   9b   10i

12. THE PENAL LAWS

a) Besides   b) made   c) prohibiting   d) subordinate   e) these   f) author
g) encouraged   h) against   i) brighter

13. THE FRENCH IN IRELAND
1.

Is a bhfaighimid fós ár saoirse?	=	And will we get our freedom?
Ars an tSean-bhean bhocht.	=	Says the poor old woman

....

Beimid saor 'dir bhun is craobh	=	We'll be free 'tween base (of tree) and branch
Beimid saor ó thaobh go taobh	=	We'll be free from side to side
Saor go deo le cabhair na naomh!	=	Free forever with the help of the saints!

2. a) from   b) where   c) himself   d) own   e) hid   f) addressed   g) plans
   h) hanged   i) displayed

14. DANIEL O'CONNELL
a) set out   b) turn up   c) give in   d) turn out   e) called off   f) carry on

15. THE GREAT FAMINE
1. 1. illness   2. poverty   3. starvation   4. readiness   5. destination
   6. organisation   7. emigration   8. distribution   9. short-sightedness
   10. charity   11. substitution   12. scarcity   13. homelessness
   14. population   15. eviction

2. 1. Indian corn was imported.   2. Soup kitchens were set up.
   3. Workhouses had been built.   4. Grain was also grown.
   5. The cash crop was still being exported.   6. It could be said.
   7. Most of the seed potatoes had been eaten.   8. No rent was being
      collected.   9. Many Famine memorials have been erected.

3. a) leaves   b) within   c) seen   d) spread   e) relied   f) there   g) made
   h) until   i) weather   j) crops

4. a) forced   b) journey   c) later   d) Although   e) little   f) famine

VOCABULARY REVIEW, CHAPTERS 11-15
   volunteer   suspect   mole   seaweed

   trail   rot   fear   persuade

   Inquisition   ban   struggle   grain

   drought   wage   barn   subscription

16. THE FENIANS
1. a) 1   b) 3   c) 6   d) 5   e) 8   f) 2   g) 4   h) 7   i) 1   j) 5   k) 3   l) 2
   m) 4

2. a) rights   b) thrown   c) raise   d) founded   e) against   f) alliance
   g) become   h) skill   i) topic

17. PARNELL

1. 1e 2i 3j 4g 5h 6b 7a 8d 9f 10c

2. a) navy b) at c) ironic d) disruption e) condemned f) means
g) will h) contested i) filed j) deteriorated

3. a) 45 b) 76 c) 22 d) 1776

18. THE GAELIC REVIVAL

True: 1, 3, 4, 5 (it may be punched away), 7 (Cuchulain), 8 (The Brown Bull of Cooley), 9 (from *The Playboy of the Western World*), 11 and 12.
False: 2, 6 and 10.

19. THE 1916 RISING

1. a) services b) trying c) disguised d) followed e) appear
f) distracted g) reached h) fool i) off j) that k) before

2. 2e 3n 4i 5a 6j 7f 8k 9o 10m 11c 12b 13g 14l 15p 16h

20. THE WAR OF INDEPENDENCE

1. A rough drawing of the line dividing the 6 counties from the rest of the island (the separate county lines themselves are not required).

2. 1c 2h 3d 4f 5b 6j 7e 8g 9a 10i

3. a) imprisoned b) escape c) key d) While e) them f) envious/jealous
g) sent h) go i) would j) himself

VOCABULARY REVIEW, CHAPTERS 16-20

scaffold funds movement split

affair publish tolerate sympathetic

propose frustrated sentence envious

duplicate ballad unify jeer

21. THE CIVIL WAR

1. a) held b) contender c) promoters d) reprisal e) keeping
f) out g) celebrating h) cables i) ring j) fight

2. (Erskine Childers)
a) born b) brought c) imported d) award
e) made f) negotiators g) opposed h) return i) killing
j) executed k) accused l) execution m) possession

(Kevin O'Higgins)
n) both o) imprisoned p) man q) revolution
r) over s) including t) forgave

22. FREE STATE AND REPUBLIC

a) welcomed   b) territory   c) pragmatically/practically   d) dropped
e) reason   f) already   g) strict   h) condemned

23. NORTHERN IRELAND

1.

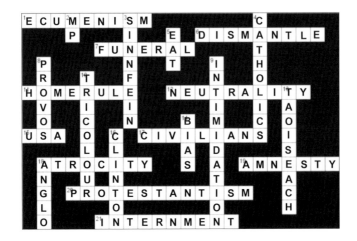

2. 1) Sinn Féin   2) UDR – Ulster Defence Regiment   3) UVF – Ulster Volunteer Force   4) Provos – Provisional IRA   5) UDA – Ulster Defence Association   6) SDLP – Social Democratic and Labour Party
7) UUP – Ulster Unionist Party   8) INLA – Irish National Liberation Army
9) Real/New IRA   10) DUP – Democratic Unionist Party   11) RUC – Royal Ulster Constabulary

VOCABULARY REVIEW, CHAPTERS 21-24

infant   mortgage   atheist   ban

isolated   atrocities   binge drinking   swear

campaign   best man   unarmed   consequently

aspiration   venue   compromise   corporate